# Physical Characteristics of Scottish Deerhound

(from the American Kennel Club breed .

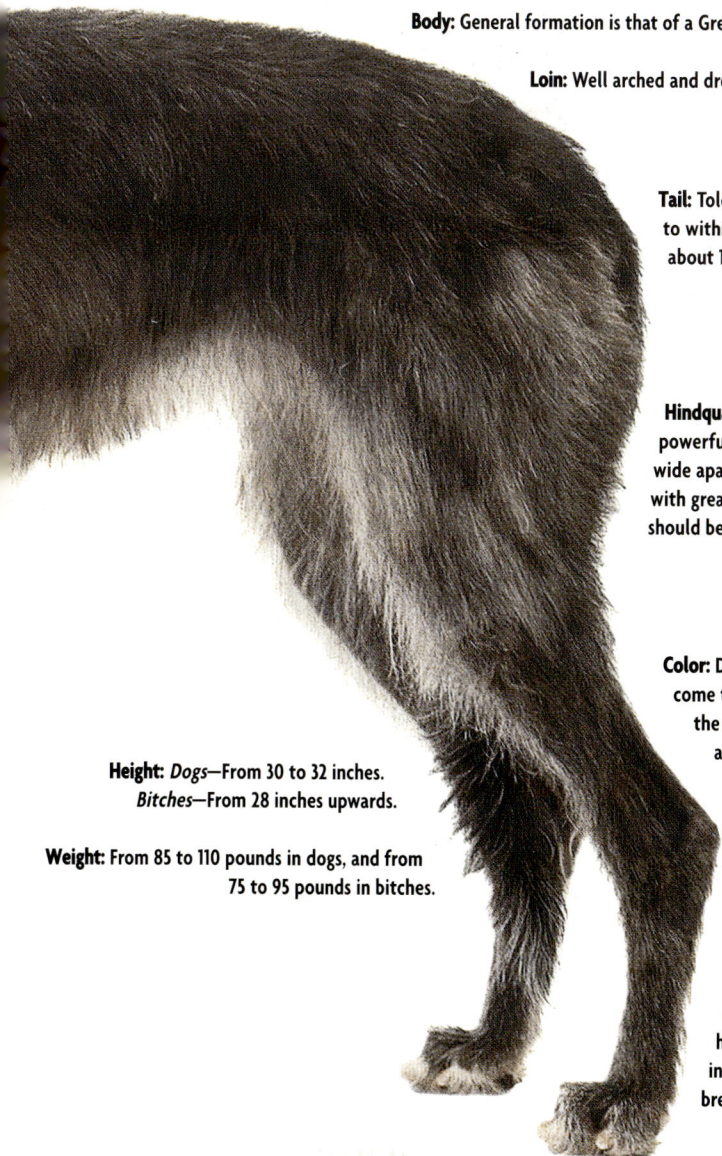

**Body:** General formation is that of a Greyhound of larger size and bone.

**Loin:** Well arched and drooping to the tail.

**Tail:** Tolerably long, tapering and reaching to within 1.5 inches of the ground and about 1.5 inches below the hocks.

**Hindquarters:** Drooping, and as broad and powerful as possible, the hips being set wide apart. The stifles should be well bent with great length from hip to hock, which should be broad and flat.

**Color:** Dark blue-gray is most preferred. Next come the darker and lighter grays or brindles, the darkest being generally preferred. Yellow and sandy red or red fawn, especially with black ears and muzzles, are equally high in estimation.

**Height:** *Dogs*—From 30 to 32 inches. *Bitches*—From 28 inches upwards.

**Weight:** From 85 to 110 pounds in dogs, and from 75 to 95 pounds in bitches.

**Coat:** The hair on the body, neck and quarters should be harsh and wiry about 3 or 4 inches long; that on the head, breast and belly much softer.

# Scottish Deerhound

◇

*By Juliette Cunliffe*

## 9     **History of the** Scottish Deerhound

Travel through antiquity to discover the true origins of this age-old sighthound from Scotland. From early written references to historical accounts by early promoters of this breed, trace the rise of this fashionable rough-haired hound at the side of Queen Victoria, its presence at the shows in England, the struggles of early breeders and the breed's exportation to American shores.

## 31     **Characteristics of the** Scottish Deerhound

Discover whether the Scottish Deerhound is the right dog for you. Learn about the breed's personality, its sizable requirements, amicability with other pets and children and much more. The potential owner is also made aware of the various hereditary problems known in the breed that concern breeders and owners today.

## 40     **Breed Standard for the** Scottish Deerhound

Learn the requirements of a well-bred Scottish Deerhound by studying the description of the breed set forth in the American Kennel Club standard. Both show dogs and pets must possess key characteristics as outlined in the breed standard.

## 48     **Your Puppy** Scottish Deerhound

Find out about how to locate a well-bred Scottish Deerhound puppy. Discover which questions to ask the breeder and what to expect when visiting the litter. Prepare for your puppy-accessory shopping spree. Also discussed are home safety, the first trip to the vet, socialization and solving basic puppy problems.

## 66     **Proper Care of Your** Scottish Deerhound

Cover the specifics of taking care of your Scottish Deerhound every day: feeding for the puppy, adult and senior dog; grooming, including coat care, ears, eyes, nails and bathing; and exercise needs for your dog. Also discussed are the essentials of dog identification.

## 80     **Training Your** Scottish Deerhound

Begin with the basics of training the puppy and adult dog. Learn the principles of house-training the Scottish Deerhound, including the use of crates and basic scent instincts. Get started by introducing the pup to his collar and leash and progress to the basic commands. Find out about obedience classes and other activities.

# Contents

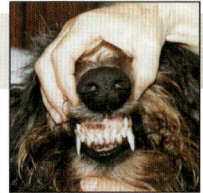

KENNEL CLUB BOOKS® **SCOTTISH DEERHOUND**
**ISBN: 1-59378-293-4**

Copyright © 2005 • Kennel Club Books, LLC
308 Main Street, Allenhurst, NJ 07711 USA
Cover Design Patented: US 6,435,559 B2 • Printed in South Korea

Photography by Carol Ann Johnson
with additional photographs by:

Dave and John Ashbey, Paulette Braun, T.J. Calhoun, Alan and Sandy Carey, Carolina Biological Supply, Juliette Cunliffe, Isabelle Français, Bill Jonas, Dr. Dennis Kunkel, Tam C. Nguyen, Phototake, Jean Claude Revy, Kent Standerford, Steve Surfman and Alice van Kempen.

**Illustrations by Patricia Peters.**

The publisher wishes to thank all of the owners whose dogs are illustrated in this book, including Jennifer Cooper, Juliette Cunliffe, Carol Ann Johnson and Glenis & Mick Peach.

*The Deer Stalkers* by Landseer, engraved by Finden, shows deer hunters with their Scottish Deerhounds in Scotland during the 1800s.

# HISTORY OF THE
# SCOTTISH DEERHOUND

The Deerhound of Scotland hunts primarily by sight and owes its origin to the Greyhound of England. Through the centuries there have been various rough-coated Greyhounds, and the Scottish Deerhound has sometimes been confused with the Irish Wolfhound. However, there is a substantial difference between these two breeds, with the Wolfhound possessing a much heavier frame and the Scottish Deerhound carrying a head that is closer to that of the Greyhound.

The Scottish Deerhound is a breed of great antiquity. It is likely that the breed was kept in Scotland in the middle of the 16th century, and there are references to dogs of Scottish Deerhound type in subsequent centuries. In 1637 Aldrovandus showed a dog clearly resembling the breed, but he called it a "White Hairy Greyhound." He did not mention that the dog was from Scotland, even though he had referred to other dogs from that area. However, a drawing by Abraham Hondius, dated 1682, very clearly depicts a Scottish Deerhound.

The Scottish
Deerhound is a
very old breed,
with evidence of
Scottish
Deerhound-type
dogs dating back
to the 16th
century.

The Scottish Deerhound is a very old breed, with evidence of Scottish Deerhound-type dogs dating back to the 16th century.

Written evidence of the breed first appeared in 1769 when Thomas Pennant visited Gordon Castle. He describes a large dog, covered with long hair and used by the Scottish chiefs in stag chases. This he called "the true Highland Greyhound" and commented that the breed had by then become very scarce.

We learn from Ralph Beilby's *A General History of Quadrupeds* (1790) that what he called the "Scottish Highland Greyhound or Wolfdog" had at one time been used by Scottish chieftains in their grand hunting parties. We can see that this splendid breed, "its eyes half hid in hair," was certainly on the decline, for

Beilby mentioned one that had been seen some years previously. Its body was strong, muscular and covered with harsh wiry reddish hair, mixed with white. According to the *Encyclopedia Britannica*, only a year later the "Highland Gre-hound" had become very scarce, but mention is made of

## A BREED OF MANY NAMES

The Scottish Deerhound has acquired many names through its history. In the UK, it is called simply Deerhound. Other names that are no longer used include the Scotch Greyhound, Rough Greyhound, Irish Wolf Dog and Highland Deerhound.

this breed's being as fierce as the Bloodhound and with as "sagacious nostrils."

## SIR WALTER SCOTT'S MAIDA

For many people, the first Scottish Deerhound that springs immediately to mind is Sir Walter Scott's Maida. In fact, Maida had a Scottish Deerhound dam and a Pyrenean sire, the latter giving some white to Maida's coat, but in most respects he looked like a Scottish Deerhound. Although Maida looked much like his dam, his sire gave him strength and power. We can learn a great deal about Maida from Washington Irving, who described this magnificent dog as "a giant in iron gray."

Maida had a grave demeanor, and most of the time acted with decorum and dignity. When the younger dogs leapt on his neck and worried his ears, he would sometimes rebuke them, but when

**CANIS LUPUS**
"Grandma, what big teeth you have!" The gray wolf, a familiar figure in fairy tales and legends, has had its reputation tarnished and its population pummeled over the centuries. Yet it is the descendants of this much-feared creature to which we open our homes and hearts. Our beloved dog, *Canis domesticus*, derives directly from the gray wolf, a highly social canine that lives in elaborately structured packs. In the wild, the gray wolf can range from 60 to 175 pounds, standing between 25 and 40 inches in height.

alone with the dogs he would play the boy as much as any of them. However, Irving felt Maida was ashamed to do so when in company and commented that he seemed to say, "Ha! Done with your nonsense, youngsters. What will the laird and that other gentleman think of me if I give way to such foolery?"

How fortunate we are today that a member of this magnificent breed was owned by a great poet like Sir Walter Scott, who used his considerable talents to render the Scottish Deerhound so memorably: "The most perfect creature of Heaven." Scott likened Maida's

Miss Norah Hartley of the Rotherwood Scottish Deerhounds not only kept accurate records of her own dogs but also housed a veritable wealth of information about the breed in her magnificent home.

This statue of Sir Walter Scott's Scottish Deerhound Maida was given to the great-, great-, great-granddaughters of Sir William Scott, Dame Jean and Patricia Maxwell-Scott.

Two Scottish Deerhounds flank the statue of Maida, under which lie his remains. Maida still guards the door of Abbotsford, where Sir Walter lived.

A scene at Abbotsford, showing Sir Walter Scott's dogs, Maida and Torrum. From a painting by Sir Edwin Landseer.

Scottish Deerhound lovers and their dogs, visiting the home of Sir Walter Scott.

In the dining room, the room in which Sir Walter Scott died overlooking his beloved River Tweed, is this small replica of Edinburgh's monument to Sir Walter, with Maida at his feet.

bark to the great guns of Constantinople: "...it takes so long to get it ready, that the smaller guns can fire off a dozen times first; but when it goes off, it plays the very devil."

Maida died peacefully in 1822, and by early in the 20th century it was believed that many of the best Scottish Deerhounds of their day were descended from him. However, when Maida died, there was something of a rumpus, for the inscription on his epitaph carried an error in Latin. This was copied in the press and vexed Scott, a man to whom the written word was so sacred. Maida was buried at the door of Abbotsford, where his remains still lie and the inscription, translated, reads:

> *Beneath the sculptured*
> *form which late you wore,*
> *Sleep soundly, Maida, at*
> *your master's door.*

Yet Maida lives on in many ways, for there is no doubt that in Scott's *Woodstock* Bevis was actually the author's favorite hound, Maida.

## ACCORDING TO SCROPE

*The Art of Deerstalking*, written by William Scrope and published in 1838, confirms how numerically weak the breed was as that time. Scrope claimed to have a perfect knowledge of every specimen of the breed in Scotland, which he thought numbered only a dozen pure Scottish Deer-

The late Patricia Maxwell-Scott (left) greets Scottish Deerhounds and their owners at the entrance gate to Abbotsford.

hounds. He was at pains to point out the differences between the Irish Wolfhound and the Scottish Deerhound, but thought that some degeneracy had taken place. This was due in part to the reduced number, but also because of neglect in crossing, selection and feeding. He believed that in earlier days Scottish Deerhounds had measured some 30 inches in height and 34 inches in girth, and weighed around 103 pounds.

Despite his belief that the breed had degenerated, Scrope still believed that no other member of the canine race had such a combination of qualities: speed, strength, size, endurance, courage, perseverance, sagacity, docility, elegance and dignity. What more can one say about the breed? Scrope has said it all!

Various attempts were made to improve the Scottish Deerhound by crossing it with other breeds but, in Scrope's opinion, all had utterly failed. Crossing with the Bulldog had added courage but had resulted in loss of speed, strength and weight. Crossing with the Bloodhound increased the power of smell, but speed and size were diminished. When the Pyrenean Wolfdog was used for the purpose of crossing, some increase in weight was produced, but both speed and courage were lost.

**SOME OF THE EARLY DOGS**
Breed enthusiasts today are fortunate indeed that through the centuries Scottish Deerhound lovers have kept accurate records of their hounds. Scrope considered that four of the finest specimens of the breed in his time belonged to Captain McNeill of Colonsay. These were the now infamous males, Buskar and Bran, and two bitches, Runa and Cavak. Two were pale yellow in color, the others a sandy red. Although quality and length of their hair varied, all had black tips to their ears, and their eyes and muzzles were black. Important too was that each of them was a uniform color, something Scrope considered an indication of purity.

**KANGAROO DOGS**
In Australia, Scottish Deerhound blood has been infused with that of the Greyhound to create Kangaroo Dogs, also sometimes known as Staghounds. Kangaroo Dogs have for decades been fast enough to catch game for their owners, and have also been strong enough to kill dingoes that have attacked the flocks. Kangaroo Dogs have been exhibited at Australia's Royal Agricultural Shows.

The Royal Art Collection features the Landseer painting entitled *The Deer Drive*. In this section of the painting, note the hunters holding their Scottish Deerhounds.

Buskar was measured and weighed in 1836, his height recorded as 71 cm (28 inches) and his weight in running condition as 38.5 kg (85 lb). Scrope noted a remarkable difference in size between dogs and bitches, a difference he thought more remarkable than in any other species of canine.

Another valuable comparison made by Scrope was the difference in measurements between a Scottish Deerhound and a fully-grown stag. No wonder, he said, that few dogs, if any, were capable of bringing down a stag single-handedly. A stag's height at the shoulder was almost 48 inches, and the extreme height from the top of the antlers to the ground was 7 feet 10 inches. As he fell, this particular stag weighed 310 pounds.

In the Highlands of Scotland, dark-gray-colored coats had been

## FROM HUNTER TO PET

Despite there having been 60 deer forests in Britain, shortly before World War I only 6 remained in which Scottish Deerhounds were kept for sporting purposes. In the words of Robert Leighton, "...the inventions of the modern gunsmith have robbed one of the grandest of hunting dogs of his glory, relegating him to the life of a pedestrian pet..."

more prevalent than the yellowish or reddish colors, but gray coats were generally softer and more woolly than the latter.

## THE SCOTTISH GREYHOUND

Like Scrope, John Meyrick was a 19th-century author from whom we learn much about the Scottish Deerhound. In 1861 he wrote about Queen Victoria's Scottish Deerhound, commenting that he knew of no other pure-bred Scottish Deerhound in the country. In his opinion, some were called Scottish Deerhounds but they were in fact Scottish Greyhounds, although some undoubtedly had some true Scottish Deerhound blood. Others were crossed with the Bloodhound or some other breed.

There continue to be differences of opinion as to whether the Scottish Greyhound and the Scottish Deerhound were, in fact, one and the same, but Meyrick informed his readers that although the former resembled the Scottish Deerhound in both color and shape, it was considerably smaller. Most Scottish Greyhounds were below 26 inches in height.

## A FASHIONABLE HOUND

Queen Victoria was a great lady whose opinions influenced the entire world, including the world

The head of a Scottish Deerhound, sketched in the early 1800s.

## PURE-BRED PURPOSE

Given the vast range of the world's 400 or so pure breeds of dog, it's fair to say that domestic dogs are the most versatile animal in the kingdom. From the tiny 1-pound lap dog to the 200-pound guard dog, dogs have adapted to every need and whim of their human masters. Humans have selectively bred dogs to alter physical attributes like size, color, leg length, mass and skull diameter in order to suit our own needs and fancies. Dogs serve humans not only as companions and guardians but also as hunters, exterminators, shepherds, rescuers, messengers, warriors, babysitters and more!

of pure-bred dogs. Several breeds owe something of their revival to the fact that Her Majesty owned the breed, thereby bringing it to public attention.

Scottish Deerhounds were kept in Queen Victoria's kennels at both Windsor and Sandringham, where they were cared for by Mr. Cole. Indeed, this gentleman became so connected with Her Majesty's hounds that some dogs became known as the "Mr. Cole breed." When the Queen and Prince Albert were in residence at Balmoral, they had with them Solomon, Hector and Bran. Bran became wonderfully famous, for he was depicted in Landseer's painting *High Life.* He

This well-known head portrait was popular with Scottish Deerhound lovers in the 1920s.

was reputed to be an exception-
ally fine dog, standing over 30
inches at the shoulder. Another
particularly famous Scottish
Deerhound belonging to the
Queen was Keildar, who was used
for hunting deer in Windsor Park.

**THE 19TH CENTURY DRAWS TO
ITS CLOSE**

By the end of the 19th century,
the Scottish Deerhound was somewhat smaller in size, with only a
few larger dogs to be found. One
of these was Lord Bredalbane's
King of the Forest, who stood 33
inches tall.

Upon his return from India,
Captain George Augustus Graham
had set up his own kennel of
Scottish Deerhounds, where he
intended, as he put it, to "rebuild"
the Irish Wolfhound. In February
1870 he purchased from Mr. Cole's
widow the Scottish Deerhound
Keildar, who had been renowned
for hunting deer at Windsor and
was described as one of the most
elegant and aristocratic-looking
Scottish Deerhounds ever seen.
This was an interesting introduction to his kennel, for this dog had
as a grandsire a black Russian
Wolfhound. Also in the pedigree

The champion of champions in her time, St. Ronan's Rhyme, born February 23, 1903. It was written that she was "probably the most perfect dog of any breed at present living."

Misses Loughrey's Idric of Ross (left) and Eng. Ch. Phorp of the Foothills at England's prestigious Crufts show in 1934. "Phorp" won first prize and was awarded Best Scottish Deerhound in the show.

## SCOTTISH DEERHOUNDS AT EARLY ENGLISH SHOWS

At the first Manchester Dog Show, held at Bellvue Zoological Gardens in 1861, the Scottish Deerhound was one of only a few breeds that were separately classified, albeit with only one class. By 1863, Scottish Deerhounds had mustered up a "fair entry" and that same year at the Birmingham Show, the Duke of Beaufort took along some Scottish Deerhounds, among other breeds, and came away with several prizes.

In 1869 Queen Victoria exhibited four of her Scottish Deerhounds at Islington in London, and indeed the breed continued to be scheduled with some consistency throughout the next decade.

was Tank, a dog bought by Mr. Cole from Tankerville Castle in 1858.

Size was a constant topic of conversation, and in 1872 an informative list of heights was published. Most of the males measured 28 inches, the smallest just half an inch less and the largest 30.5 inches. The tallest of the bitches measured 26 inches; none was smaller, but one was 29 inches.

Undoubtedly, in the mid-19th century Scottish Deerhounds were varied indeed. Some had good hard coats, others had woolly ones, almost resembling the coat of a sheep. Indeed, even today, faulty coat textures come through from time to time, the worst of them

Revis of Rotherwood was a fine example of Miss Norah Hartley's quality Scottish Deerhound breeding.

By the 1880s Captain Graham had drawn up a list of the most notable Scottish Deerhounds of the previous hundred years. Of these, Torrum seems to have been the most notable stud dog, described as a "grand specimen of his race, strong framed, with plenty of hair of a blue brindle color."

E. Watson Bell's book, published in 1892, expressed the author's opinion that the judges of his day had "fads." Bell made some interesting comments about the eye of the Scottish Deerhound, which, he said, should resemble the "eye of the terrier as nearly as possible." He had been given this description of the eye by an experienced old breeder, but such an eye had almost been lost due to the crosses made with the Bulldog and Bloodhound. The small eye,

known as "woollies." There were certainly some dogs that were full of quality, but others were very coarse, and some poor specimens of the breed gained their championship titles, a happening that rarely occurs in Britain today.

Ernest G. Chapman drew this head study to show prominent features of the Scottish Deerhound: harsh strong coat, gentleness of eye, small ear and fine long lines of the muzzle.

he considered, was of great use to the breed, for it enabled the dog to see a greater distance than did a round one.

By then the breed was laboring under a mixture of strains; breeders were so confused that they were producing many different kinds of Scottish Deerhounds. Although the black smooth-eared dog had a most striking appearance, this somewhat detracted from the shaggy, rough, Highland tyke-like look that was characteristic of the breed.

## SCOTTISH DEERHOUND COLOR

As the dog world moved into the 20th century, the color favored by breeders for Scottish Deerhounds on the show bench was dark blue or gray brindle, though in earlier years the light fawn color had been more desirable. The reason that the lighter Scottish Deerhounds had been preferred was said to have been because they could more easily be seen on the hillside.

Many colors were bred just before the century turned, including blue brindle, fawn brindle, red brindle, red, fawn, sandy and

It was written that "there is no more docile breed than the Scottish Deerhound," as shown by this young Deerhound and his young mistress.

Some of Miss Hartley's Scottish Deerhounds. Like all breeds in the Greyhound family, Scottish Deerhounds carry their tails in the characteristic manner.

**CLUB TO THE RESCUE!**
The Deerhound Club has always helped its members through difficult times. During World War II, several Scottish Deerhounds were "evacuated" to breed enthusiasts living in less dangerous rural areas. About 16 breeders managed to keep stock through the war years, and by the end of 1944 there was still an enthusiastic band ready to carry on.

"almost black and white." White, though, was not considered an acceptable color within the breed, for it denoted crossbreeding. White markings were considered a sign of impure blood, although a little white on toes and chest was "passable."

### THE DEERHOUND CLUB

In 1892 the Deerhound Club was formed in Britain (the breed's name in Britain is simply Deerhound). Even today, this is the only club for this breed recognized by England's Kennel Club. Thanks to the Deerhound Club, the crosses came to a halt, and a standard of breed points was drawn up, which was endorsed at a meeting held in Shrewsbury in June 1901. Whether or not it was right to have curtailed crosses was a matter for debate, for the breed by then had not yet fully recovered. However, the breed just about managed to hold its own in the years that followed.

Since then, the Scottish Deerhound has remained in the hands of some highly dedicated breeders, and some notable dogs have achieved very high honors in the show ring. The breed is still not particularly numerically strong, but the Scottish Deerhound is a very special breed and genuine enthusiasts are happy to keep it that way.

### SCOTTISH DEERHOUNDS IN THE UNITED STATES

Bonnie Robin was the first Scottish Deerhound registered with the AKC in 1886. The breed standard was based on the English standard, with a few minor variations. A white blaze on the forehead and a white collar are reasons for disqualification in the US, whereas in Britain they are only considered "unacceptable."

Scottish Deerhounds are not used on antlered game in the US, since it is illegal to hunt deer or other antlered game with dogs. However, the breed has been effective on other game, such as coyotes, wolves and rabbits.

The national parent club is the Scottish Deerhound Club of America, whose purpose is to safeguard the breed and its best interests in the US. It publishes its official newsletter, *The Claymore*, six times per year. It contains information about the breed in the US as well as Canada, Europe and beyond, as well as helpful infor-

**Ch. Timber of Gayleward, owned and bred by Gayle Bontecou.**

mation about health and husbandry, litter announcements and future events, such as national and regional specialties, breed seminars and lure coursing.

In 1994 the AKC held its inaugural National Lure Coursing Championship in Mt. Holly, New Jersey. This was won by a 14-month-old Scottish Deerhound.

The Deerhound has a loyal following in the US, and although entries at all-breed shows are not usually high, enthusiasts and their hounds come out in force at specialty shows.

The US and Canada are large countries and have many dedicated followers of this wonderful breed. Kate Lyons of the Lyonhil kennel in Ohio is the US's longest continuous breeder of Deerhounds, acquiring her first hound, Ch. Jeffcairn Dylna, known fondly as "Dilly," in 1958. Lyons has been breeding successfully for more than 40 years, and it was Dilly who produced her first litter of Deerhound puppies on January 7, 1963. (This was not just any litter either—there were 15 puppies!) Lyons has been showing Deerhounds for around 30 years, although she took a 10-year break to show her Morgan horses.

It is Lyons's feeling that the most important wins occur when a Deerhound competes against his own breed for Best of Breed, so her hounds do not always compete in the Group ring. Even so, the first ever American-bred Scottish Deerhound to win a Best in Show award was Ch. Lyonhil Highland Fling, home-bred and owner-handled by Lyons. Because of the breed's quiet, gentle temperament, Lyons feels that the Scottish Deerhound makes an ideal pet, but is unsuited for kennel life.

Gayle Bontecou is well known for her Gayleward Deerhounds and is undoubtedly one of the most prominent breeders in the US. Paula Pascoe and Grant Winchell are known for their successful Lehigh kennel and used one of Bontecou's young dogs, Ch. Gayleward's Tiger, to produce a litter out of their own Ch. Lehigh Yanna. Scottish Deerhounds from this kennel are actively campaigned and have won a whole string of victories. Janet Porter of the d'Lux kennel in Virginia has also had considerable success with

Ch. Gayleward's Timber II, owned and bred by Gayle Bontecou.

her Deerhounds and is a board member of the Scottish Deerhound Club of America (SDCA).

There are several other American Scottish Deerhound kennels worthy of note. Ray and Jana Brinlee's Jaraluv hounds have indeed made their mark, and the late Karen Colisimo's Ayr kennel was influential for some time. Jeanne Frye of Ohio has had her Thistleglen Deerhounds for a long while, and Sally Poole's Windshift Deerhounds cannot go without mention. The list of US Scottish Deerhound enthusiasts goes on,

with the following all worthy of mention: Norma and the late Robert Sellers (Vale Vue), Joan Shagan (Jubalhil), Frances Smith and Wendy Fast (Dhu Mor) Shay Rhinlander (Pibroch), the late Maurie Lewis (Highstone), the late Frieda and Paul Pilat (Shanid) and Ceil and Scott Dove (Foxcliffe).

Scottish Deerhounds have also been bred in Canada with considerable success. Barbara Heidenreich has lived with Deerhounds for 35 years, during which time she has enjoyed many

Ch. Gayleward's Mini Ha Ha, owned and bred by Gayle Bontecou.

Ch. Gayleward's Pollyanna, owned and bred by Gayle Bontecou.

Am./Can. Ch. Crannoch's Fenris O'Fern Hill had a brilliant show and coursing career, leaving a legacy of longevity and versatility. There have been so many great hounds at Fernhill kennels that it would be impossible to mention them all, but Barbara considers her most beautiful Deerhound ever to be Am./Can. Ch. Fernhill's Espirit who produced many superb puppies and lived to a ripe old age. Fernhill hounds have been all-breed Best in Show winners in Canada, the US and Mexico, and this notable kennel has produced several specialty Best in Show winners.

Other successful Deerhound breeders in Canada are Peter Balitzer of Dunkeld kennels and Jay and Elin Phinzy of Black North kennels. Sheila Matheson shows dogs from her Pennant kennel with many impressive wins to her credit, among them a big winner from Fernhill.

coursing triumphs and show successes. Barbara treasures the opportunity to watch her hounds in full flight over the 200 acres of field at Fernhill kennels. Some of her Deerhounds have been used for hunting purposes domestically and abroad. Several of the Fernhill Deerhounds have had success in the hands of other owners. One is Margaret Sudekum's Dual Ch. Fernhill's Electra at Fitzhugh, who is not only a conformation champion but also an excellent lure courser, even as a veteran. Barbara attributes her hounds' effortless trotting, though many generations have since come and gone, to her Am./Can. Ch. Gwent's Trefor O'Fern Hill, whose grandson

**BETH GELERT**

The story of Beth Gelert surely ranks among one of the most loved canine poems ever written. Deerhound enthusiasts say that Beth Gelert was a Scottish Deerhound, but Irish Wolfhound followers lay claim to him, too! Sadly, the story is only fable. In fact, there are strong similarities between this story and folklore of other European countries as well as India.

Ch. Gayleward's
Grey Gucci, owned
and bred by
Gayle Bontecou.

Ch. Gayleward's
Jaraluv Nike
owned and bred
by Gayle Bontecou.

The author having a chat with her Scottish Deerhound. Along with being friendly and docile, the Scottish Deerhound also seems to be a great listener!

# CHARACTERISTICS OF THE

# SCOTTISH DEERHOUND

There is something very special about the Scottish Deerhound that attracts genuine devotees. This is a breed that immediately conjures up images of the life it used to lead in baronial halls and out stalking deer in the Scottish Highlands. Times have changed, but in essence the Scottish Deerhound has not. This is truly a grand animal, a dog that carries himself with quiet dignity.

Those of us who adore the breed seem to be besotted by these dogs, and understandably so. However, this is most certainly not the breed for everyone. The Scottish Deerhound is of great size, and though one can sometimes take up surprisingly little space when curled up in a ball, he can look very different when sprawled across your sofa, sleeping in front of the fireplace or roaming at table-height around the kitchen or dining room!

A Scottish Deerhound requires space, exercise and a certain amount of strength. Although for years many female Scottish Deerhound owners, some of them elderly, have made a remarkable sight walking with several well-behaved Scottish Deerhounds, it should always be remembered that these ladies have in many cases almost grown up with these hounds. They know how to handle them and how to gain and keep their respect. Such a relationship is not achieved overnight! An unprepared owner, male or female, is likely to be the one taken for a walk.

Another thing to consider is that the Scottish Deerhound, being a large dog, requires much more food than one of the smaller breeds. He can accelerate quickly and run fast, so he also needs a suitable yard or paddock with a secure high fence. Moreover, owners should bear in mind that although they may love large dogs, not everyone does. Although unlikely to intend any harm, an enormous unrestrained Scottish Deerhound approaching a child or adult can be frightening, and there is always the possibility that someone frail could be bowled over inadvertently!

## PERSONALITY
Keen in the field and gentle in the home, the Scottish Deerhound should have a friendly temperament. The breed should be docile

and good-tempered. These aspects of its personality are very important features of the breed, for a Scottish Deerhound is a large, powerful animal; if temperament were not easy, the breed would be very difficult to handle. Unfortunately, there can be the very occasional exception, but in general Scottish Deerhounds live up to their breed standard's requirements regarding temperament. They should never be suspicious, aggressive or nervous.

Any indication of ill temper should be dealt with at the very first sign. This must be corrected immediately and firmly, so that the Scottish Deerhound always knows who is in charge. This is a breed that is obedient, and is therefore easy to train because of its will to please. The late Miss Norah Hartley of the Rotherwood hounds described the Scottish

> **A REMEDY FOR WAX**
> When candle wax has dripped somewhere it shouldn't have, it can be removed by rubbing with a wad of Scottish Deerhound hair. The wax clings to the hound's hair, and this solution to the problem apparently does not damage even a fine antique finish.

Deerhound as "obedient and gentle, trusting and unsuspicious." She thought, too, that the breed was always ready to provide companionship to those who valued those qualities. How right she was! A Scottish Deerhound undoubtedly seems to understand the mood of his owner, rejoicing in the gaiety of happiness yet noticing the sobriety of less joyful times and responding accordingly.

## DEERHOUNDS AND OTHER PETS

Many Scottish Deerhound owners are devoted only to the breed and choose not to keep any other type of dog. However, there are other owners who keep them alongside other breeds and, managed sensibly, this need not present a problem. In my own experience, my Scottish Deerhound enjoyed the company of other dogs, both large and small. Having said that, when a Scottish Deerhound is in the company of small breeds, I am always aware of the damage that

Despite the Scottish Deerhound's size, Jemma doesn't seem to think she takes up a lot of space. The author's Scottish Deerhound relaxes in a favorite chair.

could be done if an awkward situation were allowed to get out of hand. For example, I am certainly conscious of the elderly or infirm Lhasa Apso, who would be all too ready to stand her ground when things did not quite go her way. In such circumstances I am cautious which dogs I leave alone together and which I do not.

On the other hand, I have had many a small breed who thoroughly enjoyed curling up next to a Scottish Deerhound on the sofa, resting a head comfortably on a warm gray hairy mass. In dog ownership, proper management and sensible control play large parts in the success or failure of relationships between pets.

Many Scottish Deerhounds are reputed to chase cats, and to kill them if given half the chance. Again, there are exceptions, and if carefully introduced a hound will live, as mine have, in peace with the family cat. Whether or not that same Scottish Deerhound would look so favorably on a strange cat taking a shortcut through his yard might be quite another matter! With my even-tempered Scottish Deerhounds, I even kept a pet Angora rabbit, but never, never would I let the rabbit meet these sighthounds nose to nose!

## DEERHOUNDS WITH CHILDREN
Anyone whose dogs come into close contact with children must

**HEART-HEALTHY**
In this modern age of ever-improving cardio-care, no doctor or scientist can dispute the advantages of owning a dog to lower a person's risk of heart disease. Studies have proven that petting a dog, walking a dog and grooming a dog all show positive results toward lowering your blood pressure. The simple routine of exercising your dog—going outside with the dog and walking, jogging or playing catch—is heart-healthy in and of itself. If you are normally less active than your physician thinks you should be, adopting a dog may be a smart option to improve your own quality of life as well as that of another creature.

be sure that each treats the other with respect. This is of particular importance in the case of a dog as large as a Scottish Deerhound who could undoubtedly do damage to a child, albeit in error or in play. Children can often engage dogs in their games, encouraging them to become unruly and overly-excited. This might be good fun while it lasts, but a quick and unexpected upward movement of a Scottish Deerhound's head can all too easily do damage, or a Scottish Deerhound jumping up can easily knock over a child.

Scottish Deerhounds are tolerant animals and most of them enjoy the company of children, especially if they have been sensibly introduced while the dog is still young. Nevertheless, like all dogs, Scottish Deerhounds do appreciate some peace and quiet, and the limits of their tolerance should never be put to the test.

## SIZE

Although not as heavy as some breeds of comparable height, the Scottish Deerhound is very large and this should never be overlooked. For dogs, the minimum height at withers should be 30 inches; bitches should be at least 28 inches. Males are generally more substantially built than bitches and should weigh between 85 and 110 pounds in adulthood, while bitches when fully-grown are between 75 and 95 pounds.

There are no two ways about it: however good the temperament, a Scottish Deerhound is a powerful dog, strong enough and with sufficient endurance to pull down a stag. When considering ownership of a Scottish Deerhound, it is essential always to bear this in mind and to be certain that your personal and family situation, as well as your home environment, are suitable for a dog of this strength and size.

**LIFESPAN**
In general, large breeds do not live as long as smaller ones, so owners should not expect a Scottish Deerhound to live well into his teens. Indeed, there are a few that do, but 10 or 11 years is a good lifespan for a Scottish Deerhound, and sadly there are some who don't make it into double digits.

Although very gentle, Scottish Deerhounds are large, strong dogs and too much for a child to handle alone. Adults must supervise child-dog interactions at all times.

## COAT AND COLOR

Although it should not be over-coated, the Scottish Deerhound is a shaggy-coated breed. The coat is thick, lying close to the body, ragged and harsh or crisp to the touch. Scottish Deerhound coats do vary though, and some need more attention than others.

Ideally the coat should be roughly 3 to 4 inches long on the body, neck and quarters, but the coat on the head, breast and belly is substantially softer. The hair on the ear is different again, this described as soft, glossy and like a mouse's coat to the touch. On the inside of both the fore- and hindlegs, there is a slightly hairy fringe.

The color of Scottish Deerhounds today seems to have somewhat less variety than in days gone by, when more light-colored hounds were recorded.

Today the majority of Scottish Deerhounds are dark blue-gray, but they may also be darker or lighter gray. In theory they may also be brindle, yellow, sandy red or red fawn with black points, but certainly the paler colors are almost never seen today.

The Scottish Deerhound is really a self-colored dog, so the less white carried in the coat, the better. However, a white chest, white toes and a slight white tip to the stern are permissible. Any evidence of a white blaze on the head or a white collar is unaccept-able in the breed and in the US will disqualify the dog from conformation competition.

## SPEED LIMIT

Because of the Scottish Deerhound's size and construc-tion, this breed can move at great speed; this should always be

The Scottish Deerhound's great speed and keen sighthound instincts make him well suited to racing and lure coursing—activities that provide great exercise and opportunity to hone the breed's natural abilities.

remembered when exercising your dog off lead. For his safety and to prevent his getting away from you, off-leash exercise should take place only in securely enclosed areas. The Scottish Deerhound is biddable, but he is still a sighthound with strong instincts. Sadly, there are frequent examples of Scottish Deerhounds having been injured or even killed when they have taken off at speed and are out of sight of their owners.

Young hounds should never be over-exercised until their period of fastest growth is complete, but an adult can readily cope with several miles each day. A combination of lead work on a hard surface coupled with free exercise should be given, and if this can be done twice a day, all the better!

## HEALTH CONSIDERATIONS

Compared with many other breeds, the Scottish Deerhound is a fundamentally healthy one, although like all dogs, some do suffer from illness. It is only fair to owners, and to the dogs themselves, that attention is paid to the problems that can occur. Veterinary research has made great strides in recent years, so owners and breeders are now more aware of problems than they were in years gone by. Knowing something about the potential problems in the breed can assist owners in knowing what to discuss with breeders and when it

will be necessary to seek veterinary advice.

### SENSITIVITY TO MEDICATION

Scottish Deerhounds, like other sighthounds, have a low proportion of body fat in relation to their size. As a result, anesthesia is one of various medications to which they are sensitive, so it is important to discuss this with your veterinarian prior to surgery taking place. A special anesthetic that is more suitable for Scottish Deerhounds and other similar breeds can be used. This avoids the risk of the anesthetic's recycling through the body, something that can have fatal results, as the author knows, sadly, only too well. Additionally,

Scottish Deerhounds are active participants in activities around the home. Author Juliette Cunliffe with her Scottish Deerhound Jemma, who enjoyed helping with the chores of rural life.

discuss safe wormers, flea preventives and antibiotics with your vet, as certain types of these cause potentially fatal reactions in Deerhounds.

**BLOOD PRESSURE AND HEART**
Blood pressure tests have provided data that Scottish Deerhounds have the highest blood pressure among the sighthound breeds. In some cases, dogs with high blood pressure suffer from dilated cardiomyopathy, a heart problem in which the heart muscle becomes feeble. This may result in poor ability to exercise, coughing, fainting, collapse, heart arrhythmia or heart failure. This does occur in Scottish Deerhounds, but is not so commonly seen as in some other large breeds. Supplementation with L-carnitine has proved helpful with dilated cardiomyopathy, and this should be discussed with your veterinarian.

**LIVER SHUNT**
All Scottish Deerhound litters should be tested for liver shunt in order to detect any affected puppies. Liver shunt is a non-inflammatory disorder that is a result of abnormal blood vessel development before birth. It produces signs similar to liver failure and is apparent in youngsters.

This problem causes liver cells to be deprived of nutrients needed to synthesize plasma proteins and other substances, hampering growth. High concentrations of ammonia remain in the blood and these high levels can affect the brain. Signs of the disease are vomiting, loss of appetite, convulsions and mental disturbance.

**BONE CANCER**
Bone cancer (osteosarcoma) more commonly affects larger breeds than smaller ones and has been cited in Scottish Deerhounds. Unfortunately, most tumors involving bone are malignant, and tumors occur particularly at the ends of the long bones. Initial signs are evident pain and lameness, with or without localized swelling. Osteosarcoma typically affects Deerhounds of age five and older, and females are at a greater risk than males.

**GASTRIC TORSION (BLOAT)**
Commonly affecting deep-chested breeds, gastric torsion, also known as bloat or gastric dilatation, is a rapid accumulation of gas and liquid in the stomach of a dog. This accumulation distends the stomach, leading to blockage of the sphincter. The stomach can also become displaced, twisting in on itself, again blocking the sphincter. This can be fatal, so immediate veterinary attention must be sought as a matter of urgency. Surgery can be success-

ful, but regrettably the post-operative death rate is quite high.

The initial sign of bloat is a distended abdomen with copious salivation and unproductive attempts to vomit. Respiratory difficulties ensue, followed by a state of shock. If tapping the abdominal wall creates a drum-like sound, this is indicative of bloat. As onset of the condition is largely related to feeding and exercise practices, it is discussed in more detail in the section on feeding.

## THYROID PROBLEMS

Tests have shown that Scottish Deerhounds often have underactive thyroids, which means that the level of the thyroid hormone in the blood is lower than would be expected. However, in Scottish Deerhounds this falls within the breed's normal range and does not, therefore, indicate a particularly high incidence of hypothyroidism. However, a dog affected

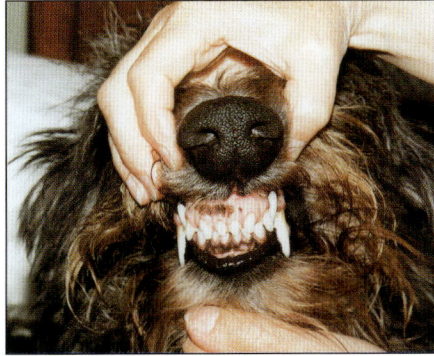

A proper healthy adult bite. Dental maintenance is an important aspect of your Scottish Deerhound's healthcare.

with hypothyroidism can be managed easily with daily medication and dietary changes.

## INJURY

The Scottish Deerhound enjoys running and is very swift. However, so engrossed is the hound with the excitement of the chase that an accident may happen. Scottish Deerhounds used in coursing frequently work on rough terrain. Wire fences are also prone to appear from nowhere! People who run their Scottish Deerhounds loose on territory unknown to them should always be on the alert for mishaps. Many of a Deerhound's injuries come from running and jumping and occur in the feet and legs. Episodes of neck pain also have been seen, but this is not necessarily injury-related. If your Deerhound does become hurt, keep him as warm and comfortable as possible while you seek help. Carry a first-aid kit for minor problems.

### HOLY WINDHOUND!

At the first sign of any minor infection, live yogurt, administered orally, can be of great benefit. This sometimes has the effect of rectifying the problem almost immediately, before a course of antibiotics becomes necessary. Feeding live yogurt for several weeks will also usually help the situation if your Scottish Deerhound is prone to passing unpleasant wind!

# BREED STANDARD FOR THE
# SCOTTISH DEERHOUND

**INTRODUCTION TO THE BREED STANDARD**

The breed standard for the Scottish Deerhound is set down by the Scottish Deerhound Club of America and approved by the American Kennel Club. Revisions are made from time to time, but only after careful study and agreement from club members. As an example, in England the standard remained virtually unchanged for around 100 years, until it was revised during the 1980s. This was not done at the request of the Deerhound Club, but of The Kennel Club, which at that time changed all breed standards to create some uniformity between them. Further, the AKC standard was last revised in 1935!

A breed standard is designed effectively to paint a picture in words, though each reader will almost certainly interpret these words slightly differently. However, reading the words alone is never enough to fully comprehend the intricacies of a breed. In addition, it is necessary for devotees to watch Scottish Deerhounds being judged at shows and, if possible, to attend breed seminars. Truly dedicated Scottish

Deerhound owners will want to give themselves every possible opportunity to absorb as much as possible about the breed they love so much.

The breed standard undoubtedly helps breeders to produce stock that comes as close to the standard as possible and helps judges to know exactly what they are looking for. In this way, to head his line of winners the judge can make a knowledgeable selection of the Scottish Deerhound that he considers to conform most closely to the breed standard.

However familiar you are with the Scottish Deerhound, it is always worth refreshing your memory by re-reading the standard, for it is sometimes too easy to conveniently forget or "overlook" certain features of the breed.

**THE AMERICAN KENNEL CLUB BREED STANDARD FOR THE SCOTTISH DEERHOUND**

**Head:** Should be broadest at the ears, narrowing slightly to the eyes, with the muzzle tapering more decidedly to the nose. The muzzle should be pointed, but the

This Scottish Deerhound was shown at the 2001 World Dog Show in Porto, Portugal. At this annual show, dogs are judged according to Fédération Cynologique Internationale (FCI) breed standards.

teeth and lips level. The head should be long, the skull flat rather than round with a very slight rise over the eyes but nothing approaching a stop. The hair on the skull should be moderately long and softer than the rest of the coat. The nose should be black (in some blue fawns—blue) and slightly aquiline. In lighter colored dogs the black muzzle is preferable. There should be a good mustache of rather silky hair and a fair beard.

## BETTER THAN THE AVERAGE DOG

Even though you may never show your dog, you should still read the breed standard. The breed standard tells you more than just physical specifications such as how tall your dog should be; it also describes how he should act, how he should move and what unique qualities make him the breed that he is. You are not investing money in a pure-bred dog so that you can own a dog that "sort of looks like" the breed you're purchasing. You want a typical, handsome representative of the breed, one that is unmistakably recognizable as the breed you've so carefully selected and researched. If the parents of your prospective puppy bear little or no resemblance to the dog described in the breed standard, you should keep searching!

**Ears:** Should be set on high; in repose, folded back like a Greyhound's, though raised above the head in excitement without losing the fold, and even in some cases semierect. A prick ear is bad. Big thick ears hanging flat to the head or heavily coated with long hair are bad faults. The ears should be soft, glossy, like a mouse's coat to the touch and the smaller the better. There should be no long coat or long fringe, but there is sometimes a silky, silvery coat on the body of the ear and the tip. On all Deerhounds, irrespective of color of coat, the ears should be black or dark colored.

**Neck and Shoulders:** The neck should be long—of a length befitting the Greyhound character of the dog. Extreme length is neither necessary nor desirable. Deerhounds do not stoop to their work like the Greyhounds. The mane, which every good specimen should have, sometimes detracts from the apparent length of the neck. The neck, however, must be strong as is necessary to hold a stag. The nape of the neck should be very prominent where the head is set on, and the throat clean cut at the angle and prominent. Shoulders should be well sloped; blades well back and not too much width between them. Loaded and straight shoulders are very bad faults.

The Scottish Deerhound must be symmetrical and never coarse, standing 28 to 32 inches or more at the shoulder.

**Tail:** Should be tolerably long, tapering and reaching to within 1.5 inches of the ground and about 1.5 inches below the hocks. Dropped perfectly down or curved when the Deerhound is still, when in motion or excited, curved, but in no instance lifted out of line of the back. It should be well covered with hair, on the inside, thick and wiry, underside longer and towards the end a slight fringe is not objectionable. A curl or ring tail is undesirable.

**Eyes:** Should be dark—generally dark brown, brown or hazel. A very light eye is not liked. The eye should be moderately full, with a soft look in repose, but a keen, far away look when the

Handlers gait their dogs in the ring so that the dogs' movement can be evaluated.

Dr. Seamus Caine's impressive champion, Killoeter Onich, pictured here after a Hound Group win.

formation being unsuited for uphill work, and very unsightly.

**Legs and Feet:** Legs should be broad and flat, and good broad forearms and elbows are desirable. Forelegs must, of course, be as straight as possible. Feet close and compact, with well-arranged toes. The hindquarters drooping, and as broad and powerful as possible, the hips being set wide apart. A narrow rear denotes lack of power. The stifles should be well bent, with great length from hip to hock, which should be broad and flat. Cowhocks, weak pasterns, straight stifles and splay feet are very bad faults.

**Coat:** The hair on the body, neck and quarters should be harsh and wiry about 3 or 4 inches long; that on the head, breast and belly much softer. There should be a slight fringe on the inside of the forelegs and hind legs but nothing approaching the "feather" of a Collie. A woolly coat is bad. Some good strains have a mixture of silky coat with the hard which is preferable to a woolly coat. The climate of the United States tends to produce the mixed coat. The ideal coat is a thick, close-lying ragged coat, harsh or crisp to the touch.

Deerhound is roused. Rims of eyelids should be black.

**Body:** General formation is that of a Greyhound of larger size and bone. Chest deep rather than broad but not too narrow or slab-sided. Good girth of chest is indicative of great lung power. The loin well arched and drooping to the tail. A straight back is not desirable, this

**Color:** Is a matter of fancy, but the dark blue-gray is most preferred. Next come the darker and lighter grays or brindles, the darkest being generally preferred. Yellow and sandy red or red fawn, especially with black ears and muzzles, are equally high in estimation. This was the color of the oldest known strains—the McNeil and Chesthill Menzies. White is condemned by all authorities, but a white chest and white toes, occurring as they do in many of the darkest-colored dogs, are not objected to, although the less the better, for the Deerhound is a self-colored dog. A white blaze on the head, or a white collar, should entirely disqualify. The less white the better but a slight white tip to the stern occurs in some of the best strains.

**Height:** *Height of Dogs*—From 30 to 32 inches, or even more if there be symmetry without coarseness, which is rare. *Height of Bitches*—From 28 inches upwards. There is no objection to a bitch being large, unless too coarse, as even at her greatest height she does not approach that of the dog, and therefore could not be too big for work as overbig dogs are.

**Weight:** From 85 to 110 pounds in dogs, and from 75 to 95 pounds in bitches.

**Points of the Deerhound, Arranged in Order of Importance:**
1. *Typical*—A Deerhound should resemble a rough-coated Greyhound of larger size and bone.
2. *Movements*—Easy, active and true.
3. As tall as possible consistent with quality.
4. *Head*—Long, level, well balanced, carried high.
5. *Body*—Long, very deep in brisket, well-sprung ribs and great breadth across hips.
6. *Forelegs*—Strong and quite straight, with elbows neither in nor out.
7. *Thighs*—Long and muscular, second thighs well muscled, stifles well bent.
8. *Loins*—Well arched, and belly well drawn up.
9. *Coat*—Rough and hard, with softer beard and brows.
10. *Feet*—Close, compact, with well-knuckled toes.
11. *Ears*—Small (dark) with Greyhoundlike carriage.
12. *Eyes*—Dark, moderately full.
13. *Neck*—Long, well arched, very strong with prominent nape.
14. *Shoulders*—Clean, set sloping.
15. *Chest*—Very deep but not too narrow.
16. *Tail*—Long and curved slightly, carried low.
17. *Teeth*—Strong and level.
18. *Nails*—Strong and curved.

**Disqualification:** *White blaze on the head, or a white collar.*

**Approved March 1935.**

A sketch of a male Scottish Deerhound, showing correct type, balance and proportion.

## MEETING THE IDEAL

The American Kennel Club defines a standard as: "A description of the ideal dog of each recognized breed, to serve as an ideal against which dogs are judged at shows." This "blueprint" is drawn up by the breed's recognized parent club, approved by a majority of its membership and then submitted to the AKC for approval.

The AKC states that "An understanding of any breed must begin with its standard. This applies to all dogs, not just those intended for showing." The picture that the standard draws of the dog's type, gait, temperament and structure is the guiding image used by breeders as they plan their programs.

The body illustrations below show faults in the Scottish Deerhound:

Flat topline; incorrect ring tail with improper high set and carriage; straight, weak rear; short neck.

"East-west" front; shallow brisket; weak, underdeveloped, tucked-under rear.

Long back, flat topline and lack of arch over loin. However, this dog does possess a strong sloping rear that provides proper propulsion.

Straight shoulders; weak pasterns; shallow chest; extreme arch over loin; dip behind shoulders; weak, under-angulated rear.

Scottish Deerhound head of correct proportions, with correct ear size and carriage.

Scottish Deerhound head in which the foreface is too short, lacking strength and substance. The topskull is domed and the stop too pronounced.

Compare this Irish Wolfhound head, which is generally more substantial.

# SCOTTISH DEERHOUND

**HOW TO SELECT A PUPPY**
Before deciding to look for a Scottish Deerhound puppy, it is essential that you fully appreciate the merits and drawbacks of the breed. You must be absolutely clear in your mind that this is the right breed for you and your family. Apart from other aspects of the breed, you will have to take into consideration size and strength, temperament, exercise, feeding and housing. You may also wish to consider taking out veterinary insurance, for vets' bills can mount up, especially for a large dog. You must always be certain that sufficient funds are available to give your dog any veterinary attention that may be needed.

You must select a puppy from a caring breeder who has given the puppies all the attention they deserve and has looked after them well. A young puppy should look well-fed, but not pot-bellied, as this might indicate worms. Take note of the eyes, which should look bright and clear, without discharge. Likewise, there should be no discharge from the nose and certainly no evidence of runny excreta. It goes without saying that the puppies should all be clean, with absolutely no evidence of parasites such as fleas or lice. Always check the bite of your selected puppy to be sure that it is neither overshot nor undershot. This may not be too noticeable on a young puppy, but will become more evident as the puppy gets older. The Scottish Deerhound should have a perfect scissors bite. Discuss with your

**A SHOW PUPPY**
If you plan to show your puppy, you must first deal with a reputable breeder who shows his dogs and has had some success in the conformation ring. The puppy's pedigree should include one or more champions in the first and second generation. You should be familiar with the breed and breed standard so you can know what qualities to look for in your puppy. The breeder's observations and recommendations also are invaluable aids in selecting your future champion. If you consider an older puppy, be sure that the puppy has been properly socialized with people and not isolated in a kennel without substantial daily human contact.

breeder how the pup's bite will mature.

It is essential that you select a breeder with the utmost care. Start by inquiring with the breed's AKC-recognized national club, the Scottish Deerhound Club of America, who can refer you to member breeders in your region. It is also a good idea to visit a

An eleven-week-old puppy, enjoying the attention!

## FINDING A QUALIFIED BREEDER

Before you begin your puppy search, ask for references from your veterinarian and other breeders to refer you to someone they believe is reputable. Responsible breeders usually raise only one or two breeds of dog. Avoid any breeder who has several different breeds or has several litters at the same time. Dedicated breeders are usually involved with a breed or other dog club. Many participate in some sport or activity related to their breed. Reputable breeders are current on hereditary health issues in the breed, have all of the necessary testing done on breeding animals and will show you documentation proving good genetic health. Just as you want to be assured of the breeder's qualifications, the breeder wants to be assured that you will make a worthy owner. Expect the breeder to interview you, asking questions about your goals for the pup, your experience with dogs and what kind of home you will provide.

show at which Scottish Deerhounds are being exhibited. This will provide you with a valuable opportunity to talk to handlers, meet various breeders and see the quality of different bloodlines.

Once you have researched and made initial contact with several breeders and have decided on the breeder with whom you feel most comfortable, it's time to visit the litter. Since you are likely to be choosing a Scottish Deerhound as a pet dog and not a show dog, you simply should select a pup that is friendly, attractive and healthy. Scottish Deerhounds generally have large litters, averaging eight puppies, so you should have plenty from which to select your pup. Likely there will be both male and female puppies available. There is not a tremendous difference between the sexes in the Scottish Deerhound. In terms

*Sighthounds are inquisitive and very alert, traits that are evident from youth.*

of size, it's big versus bigger. Of course the male, as in most breeds, is larger and stronger. Temperamentally, male puppies, at around seven months when they reach sexual maturity, can become "headstrong" and need to be clearly informed who is the king in your castle.

Breeders commonly allow visitors to see their litters by around the fifth or sixth week, and puppies leave for their new homes between the eighth and tenth week. Breeders who permit their puppies to leave early are more interested in a profit than in their puppies' well-being. Puppies need to learn the rules of the pack from their dams, and most dams continue teaching the pups manners and dos and don'ts until at least the eighth week. Likewise, breeders spend significant amounts of time with the Scottish

Deerhound toddlers so that the pups are able to interact with the "other species," i.e., humans. Given the long history that dogs and humans share, bonding between the two species is natural but must be nurtured. A well-bred, well-socialized Scottish Deerhound pup wants nothing more than to be near you and please you.

**A COMMITTED NEW OWNER**

By now you should understand what makes the Scottish Deerhound a most unique and special dog, one that you think may fit nicely into your family and lifestyle. If you have researched breeders, you should be able to recognize a knowledge-able and responsible Scottish Deerhound breeder who cares not only about his pups but also about what kind of owner you will be. If

**GETTING ACQUAINTED**

When visiting a litter, ask the breeder for suggestions on how best to interact with the puppies. If possible, get right into the middle of the pack and sit down with them. Observe which pups climb into your lap and which ones shy away. Toss a toy for them to chase and bring back to you. It's easy to fall in love with the puppy who picks you, but keep your future objectives in mind before you make your final decision.

## THE FAMILY TREE

Your puppy's pedigree is his family tree. Just as a child may resemble his parents and grandparents, so too will a puppy reflect the qualities, good and bad, of his ancestors, especially those in the first two generations. Therefore it's important to know as much as possible about a puppy's immediate relatives. Reputable and experienced breeders should be able to explain the pedigree and why they chose to breed from the particular dogs they used.

determined by observing the puppies in action within their "pack." Your breeder's expertise and recommendations are so valuable. Although you may fall in love with a bold and brassy male, the breeder may suggest that another pup would be best for you. The breeder's experience in rearing Scottish Deerhound pups and matching their temperaments with appropriate humans offers the best assurance that your pup will meet your needs and expectations. The type of puppy that you

you have completed the final step in your new journey, you have found a litter, or possibly two, of quality Scottish Deerhound pups.

A visit with the puppies and their breeder should be an education in itself. Breed research, breeder selection and puppy visitation are very important aspects of finding the puppy of your dreams. Beyond that, these things also lay the foundation for a successful future with your pup. Puppy personalities within each litter vary, from the shy and easy-going puppy to the one who is dominant and assertive, with most pups falling somewhere in between. By spending time with the puppies you will be able to recognize certain behaviors and what these behaviors indicate about each pup's temperament. Which type of pup will complement your family dynamics is best

Eleven-week-old puppy bitch Lottie, bred by Glenis Peach, with Mick Peach. Lottie soon came to be owned by the author in partnership with Carol Ann Johnson.

## PEDIGREE VS. REGISTRATION CERTIFICATE

Too often new owners are confused between these two important documents. Your puppy's pedigree, essentially a family tree, is a written record of a dog's genealogy of three generations or more. The pedigree will show you the names as well as performance titles of all dogs in your pup's background. Your breeder must provide you with a registration application, with his part properly filled out. You must complete the application and send it to the AKC with the proper fee. Every puppy must come from a litter that has been AKC-registered by the breeder, born in the US and from a sire and dam that are also registered with the AKC.

The seller must provide you with complete records to identify the puppy. The AKC requires that the seller provide the buyer with the following: breed; sex, color and markings; date of birth; litter number (when available); names and registration numbers of the parents; breeder's name; and date sold or delivered.

dependent on you for basic survival for his entire life. Beyond the basics of survival—food, water, shelter and protection—he needs much, much more. The new pup needs love, nurturing and a proper canine education to mold him into a responsible, well-behaved canine citizen. Your Scottish Deerhound's health and good manners will need consistent monitoring and regular "tune-ups," so your job as a responsible dog owner will be ongoing throughout every stage of his life. If you are not prepared to accept these responsibilities and commit to them for the next decade, possibly longer, then you are not prepared to own a dog of any breed.

Although the responsibilities of owning a dog may at times tax your patience, the joy of living with your Scottish Deerhound far outweighs the workload, and a well-mannered adult dog is worth your time and effort. Before your very eyes, your new charge will grow up to be your most loyal friend, devoted to you unconditionally.

### YOUR SCOTTISH DEERHOUND SHOPPING LIST

Just as expectant parents prepare a nursery for their baby, so should you ready your home for the arrival of your Scottish Deerhound pup. If you have the

select is just as important as your decision that the Scottish Deerhound is the breed for you.

The decision to live with a Scottish Deerhound is a serious commitment and not one to be taken lightly. This puppy is a living sentient being that will be heavy bowls. Buy adult-sized pans, as your puppy will grow into them before you know it.

necessary puppy supplies purchased and in place before he comes home, it will ease the puppy's transition from the warmth and familiarity of his mom and littermates to the brand-new environment of his new home and human family. You will be too busy to stock up and prepare your house after your pup comes home, that's for sure! Imagine how a pup must feel upon being transported to a strange new place. It's up to you to comfort him and to let your young pup know that he is going to be happy with you.

### FOOD AND WATER BOWLS
Your puppy will need separate bowls for his food and water. Stainless steel pans are generally preferred over plastic bowls since they sterilize better and pups are less inclined to chew on the metal. Heavy-duty ceramic bowls are popular, but consider how often you will have to pick up those

### THE DOG CRATE
Not all breeders recommend that Scottish Deerhounds be crate-trained, although dog owners know that there are definite merits to having their dogs acclimated to crates. If you think that crates are tools of punishment and confinement for when a dog has misbehaved, think again. Almost all trainers recommend a crate as the preferred house-training aid as well as for all-around puppy training and safety. Because dogs are natural den creatures that prefer cave-like environments, the benefits of crate use are many. The crate provides the puppy with his very own "safe house," a cozy place to sleep, take a break or seek comfort with a favorite toy; a travel aid to house your dog when on the road, at motels or at the vet's office; a training aid to help

Puppies should be friendly and inquisitive, as is this young Scottish Deerhound who introduces himself to a visiting relative.

Crates come in several types, although the wire crate and the fiberglass airline-type crate are the most popular. Both are safe and your puppy will adjust to either one, so the choice is up to you. The wire crates offer better visibility for the pup as well as better ventilation. Many of the wire crates easily fold into suit-case-size carriers. The fiberglass crates, similar to those used by the airlines for animal transport, are sturdier and more den-like. However, the fiberglass crates do not fold down and are less venti-lated than the wire crates, which can be problematic in hot weather. Some of the newer crates are made of heavy plastic mesh; they are very lightweight and fold up into slim-line suit-cases. However, a mesh crate is not suitable for a pup with manic chewing habits or a large-breed adult.

teach your puppy proper toileting habits; and a place of solitude when non-dog people happen to drop by and don't want a lively puppy—or even a well-behaved adult dog—saying hello or begging for their attention.

The three most common crate types: mesh on the right, wire on the left and fiberglass on top.

The extent to which you use your Scottish Deerhound's crate after house-training will depend on your individual dog and situa-tion. Regardless, don't bother with a puppy-sized crate. Although your Scottish Deerhound will be a wee fellow when you bring him home, he will grow up in the blink of an eye and your puppy crate will be useless. Purchase a crate that will accommodate an adult Scottish Deerhound. The adult will stand upward of 28 inches tall at the shoulder, when

## CONFINEMENT

It is wise to keep your puppy confined to a small "puppy-proofed" area of the house for his first few weeks at home. Gate or block off a space near the door he will use for outdoor potty trips. Expandable baby gates are useful to create puppy's designated area. If he is allowed to roam through the entire house or even only several rooms, it will be more difficult to house-train him.

full grown, so will require the largest crate available, about 54 inches long by 37 inches wide by 45 inches high. For the pup, a removable divider panel will create a smaller area in the crate, which helps with housebreaking and creates a cozier "den."

### BEDDING AND CRATE PADS

Your puppy will enjoy some type of soft bedding in his "room" (the crate), something he can snuggle into to feel cozy and secure. Old towels or blankets are good choices for a young pup, since he may (and probably will) have a toileting accident or two in the crate or decide to chew on the bedding material. Once he is fully trained and out of the early chewing stage, you can replace the puppy bedding with a perma-nent crate pad if you prefer. Crate pads and other dog beds run the gamut from inexpensive to high-

end doggie-designer styles, but don't splurge on the good stuff until you are sure that your puppy is reliable and won't tear it up or make a mess on it.

### PUPPY TOYS

Just as infants and older children require objects to stimulate their minds and bodies, puppies need toys to entertain their curious brains, wiggly paws and achy teeth. A fun array of safe doggie toys will help satisfy your puppy's chewing instincts and distract him from gnawing on the leg of your antique chair or your new leather sofa. Most puppy toys are cute and look as if they would be a lot of fun, but not all are necessarily safe or good for your puppy, so use caution when you go puppy-toy shopping.

Scottish Deerhound puppies are chewers, but adults only chew

When you can supervise the puppy, leave his crate door open so he can wander in and out of the crate as he chooses.

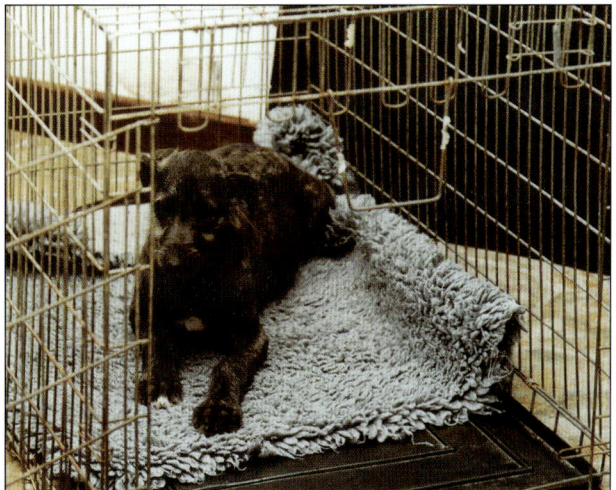

## TOYS 'R SAFE

The vast array of tantalizing puppy toys is staggering. Stroll through any pet shop or pet-supply outlet and you will see that the choices can be overwhelming. However, not all dog toys are safe or sensible. Most very young puppies enjoy soft woolly toys that they can snuggle with and carry around. (You know they have outgrown them when they shred them up!) Avoid toys that have buttons, tabs or other enhancements that can be chewed off and swallowed. Soft toys that squeak are fun, but make sure your puppy does not disembowel the toy and remove (and swallow) the squeaker. Toys that rattle or make noise can excite a puppy, but they present the same danger as the squeaky kind and so require supervision. Hard rubber toys that bounce can also entertain a pup, but make sure that the toy is too big for your pup to swallow.

when bored. The best "chewci-fiers" are nylon and hard rubber bones, which are safe to gnaw on and come in sizes appropriate for all age groups and breeds. Be especially careful of natural bones, which can splinter or develop dangerous sharp edges; pups can easily swallow or choke on those bone splinters. Veterinarians often tell of surgical nightmares involving bits of splintered bone, because in addition to the danger of choking, the sharp pieces can damage the intestinal tract. Likewise, never let your dog chew on sticks.

Similarly, rawhide chews, while a favorite of most dogs and puppies, can be equally dangerous. Pieces of rawhide are easily swallowed after they get soft and gummy from chewing, and dogs have been known to choke on large pieces of ingested rawhide. Choose the largest rawhides and not the kind with knots on the end. Remove them as soon as they start to wear down. Rawhide chews should be offered only when you can supervise the puppy or adult.

Scottish Deerhounds should only play with balls and other toys that are too large to be swallowed. They have large mouths, so they need large toys. Large marrow bones are enjoyed and are useful in loosening puppy teeth.

Soft woolly toys are special puppy favorites. They come in a wide variety of cute shapes and sizes; some look like little stuffed animals. Puppies love to shake them up and toss them about, or simply carry them around. Be careful of fuzzy toys that have button eyes or noses that your pup could chew off and swallow, and make sure that he does not disembowel a squeaky toy to remove the squeaker! Braided rope toys are similar in that they are fun to chew and toss around, but they shred easily and the strings are easy to swallow. The strings are not digestible and, if the puppy doesn't pass them in his stool, he could end up at the vet's office. As with rawhides, your puppy should be closely monitored with rope toys.

If you believe that your pup has ingested a piece of one of his toys, check his stools for the next couple of days to see if he passes the item when he defecates. At the same time, also watch for signs of intestinal distress. A call to your veterinarian might be in order to get his advice and be on the safe side.

An all-time favorite toy for puppies (young and old!) is the empty gallon milk jug. Hard plastic juice containers—46 ounces or more—are also excellent. Such containers make lots of noise when they are batted about, and puppies go crazy with delight as they play with them. However, they don't last long at all, so be

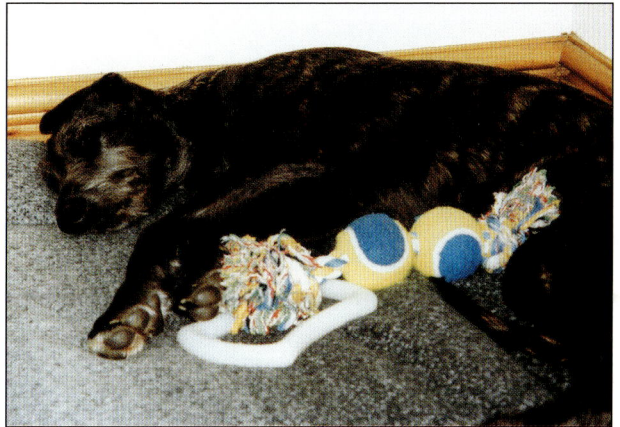

sure to remove and replace them when they get chewed up.

A word of caution about homemade toys: be careful with your choices of non-traditional play objects. Never use old shoes or socks, since a puppy cannot distinguish between the old ones on which he's allowed to chew and the new ones in your closet that are strictly off limits. That principle applies to anything that resembles something that you don't want your puppy to chew.

**COLLARS**
A lightweight nylon collar is the best choice for a very young pup. Quick-click collars are easy to put on and remove, and they can be adjusted as the puppy grows, likewise for buckle collars. Introduce him to his collar as soon as he comes home to get him accustomed to wearing it. He'll get used to it quickly and won't mind a bit. Make sure that it is

All tired out after a good chew! Chewing and napping are favorite puppy activities when he takes a break from exploring.

A young Scottish Deerhound models a sturdy yet lightweight collar attached to a light leather lead.

Who would have thought that Deerhounds start out so small? They are still a big responsibility for their mom and breeder, though.

after your pup has grown and is used to walking politely on a lead. For initial puppy walks and house-training purposes, you should invest in a shorter lead so that you have more control over the puppy. At first you don't want him wandering too far away from you, and when taking him out for toileting you will want to keep him in the specific area chosen for his potty spot.

Once the puppy is heel-trained with a traditional leash, you can consider purchasing a retractable lead. A retractable lead is excellent for walking adult dogs that are already leash-wise. This type of lead expands to allow the dog to roam farther away from you and explore a wider area when out walking, and also retracts when you need to keep him close to you. These leashes come in sizes according to weight, so be sure to purchase one that can handle an adult Deerhound.

snug enough that it won't slip off, yet loose enough to be comfortable for the pup. You should be able to slip two fingers between the collar and his neck. Check the collar often, as puppies grow in spurts, and his collar can become too tight almost overnight.

### LEASHES

A 6-foot nylon lead is an excellent choice for a young puppy. It is lightweight and not as tempting to chew as a leather lead. You can switch to a 6-foot leather lead

**HOME SAFETY FOR YOUR PUPPY**

The importance of puppy-proofing cannot be overstated. In addition to making your house comfortable for your Scottish Deerhound's arrival, you also must make sure that your house is safe for your puppy before you bring him home. There are countless hazards in the owner's personal living environment that a pup can sniff, chew, swallow or destroy. Many

are obvious; others are not. Do a thorough advance house check to remove or rearrange those things that could hurt your puppy, keeping any potentially dangerous items out of areas to which he will have access. Remember that your Scottish Deerhound pup will grow tall very quickly and not much will be out of his reach.

Electrical cords are especially dangerous, since puppies view them as irresistible chew toys. Unplug and remove all exposed cords or fasten them beneath baseboards where the puppy cannot reach them. Veterinarians and firefighters can tell you horror stories about electrical burns and house fires that resulted from puppy-chewed electrical cords. Consider this a most serious precaution for your puppy and the rest of your family.

Scout your home for tiny objects that might be seen at a pup's eye level. Keep medication bottles and cleaning supplies well out of reach, and do the same with waste baskets and other trash containers. It goes without saying that you should not use rodent poison or other toxic chemicals in any puppy area and that you must keep such containers safely locked up. You will be amazed at how many places a curious puppy can discover!

Once your house has cleared inspection, check your yard. A sturdy fence, well embedded into

## TOXIC PLANTS

Plants are natural puppy magnets, but many can be harmful, even fatal, if ingested by a puppy or adult dog. Scout your yard and home interior and remove any plants, bushes or flowers that could be even mildly dangerous. It could save your puppy's life. You can obtain a complete list of toxic plants from your veterinarian, at the public library or by looking online.

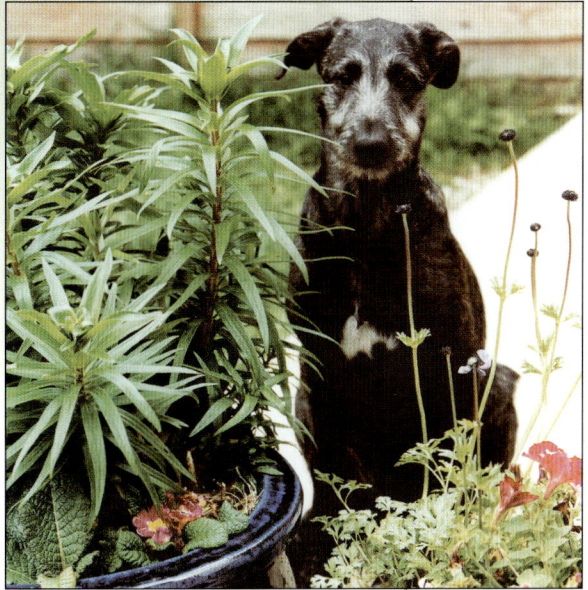

the ground, will give your dog a safe place to play and potty. Most Scottish Deerhounds are not diggers, although unspayed females may develop this habit after a heat cycle. Jumping, however, is another story. Scottish Deerhounds can jump, and you better pay attention! A fence should be at least 8 feet high to keep the Deerhound safely confined. Once a Scottish Deerhound has cleared a fence, you can be certain that this natural "wind merchant" is going to fly—and catching him will not be an easy task.

The garage and shed can be hazardous places for a dog, as things like fertilizers, chemicals and tools are usually kept there. It's best to keep these areas off limits. Antifreeze is especially dangerous to dogs, as they find the taste appealing and it takes only a few licks from the driveway to kill a dog, puppy or adult, small breed or large.

**VISITING THE VETERINARIAN**

A good veterinarian is your Scottish Deerhound puppy's best health-insurance policy. Your breeder can likely recommend a good vet in your area, someone who knows large breeds and sighthounds, or perhaps you know some other Scottish Deerhound owners who can suggest a good vet. Also arrange for your puppy's first veterinary examination beforehand, since many vets do not have appointments available immediately and your puppy should visit the vet within a day or so of coming home.

It's important to make sure your puppy's first visit to the vet is a pleasant and positive one.

**KEEP OUT OF REACH**

Most dogs don't browse around your medicine cabinet, but accidents do happen! The drug acetaminophen, the active ingredient in certain over-the-counter pain relievers, can be deadly to dogs and cats if ingested in large quantities. Acetaminophen toxicity, caused by the dog's swallowing 15 to 20 tablets, can be manifested in abdominal pains within a day or two of ingestion, as well as liver damage. If you suspect your dog has swiped a bottle of medication, get the dog to the vet immediately so that the vet can induce vomiting and cleanse the dog's stomach.

The vet should take great care to befriend the pup and handle him gently to make their first meeting a positive experience. The vet will give the pup a thorough physical examination and set up a schedule for vaccinations and other necessary wellness visits. Be sure to show your vet any health and inoculation records, which you should have received from your breeder. Your vet is a great source of canine health information, so be sure to ask questions and take notes. Creating a health journal for your puppy will make a handy reference for his wellness and any future health problems that may arise.

## FIRST NIGHT IN HIS NEW HOME

So much has happened in your Scottish Deerhound puppy's first day away from the breeder. He's had his first car ride to his new home. He's met his new human family and perhaps the other family pets. He has explored his new house and yard, at least those places where he is to be allowed during his first weeks at home. He may have visited his new veterinarian. He has eaten his first meal or two away from his dam and littermates. Surely that's enough to tire out an eight-week-old Scottish Deerhound pup—or so you hope!

It's bedtime. During the day, the pup investigated his crate, which is his new den and sleeping space, so it is not entirely strange to him. Line the crate with a soft towel or blanket that he can snuggle into and gently place him into the crate for the night. Some breeders send home a piece of bedding from where the pup slept

with his littermates, and those familiar scents are a great comfort for the puppy on his first night without his siblings.

He will probably whine or cry. The puppy is objecting to the confinement and the fact that he is alone for the first time. This can be a stressful time for you as well as for the pup. It's important that you remain strong and don't let the puppy out of his crate to comfort him. He will fall asleep eventually. If you release him, the puppy will learn that crying means "out" and will continue

Your pup may feel like a stranger in a strange land upon arrival at his new home. Don't worry, allow him to adapt at his own pace, and he quickly will become one of the family.

### THE FIRST FAMILY MEETING

Your puppy's first day at home should be quiet and uneventful. Despite his wagging tail, he is still wondering where his mom and siblings are! Let him make friends with other members of the family on his own terms; don't overwhelm him. You have a lifetime ahead to get to know each other!

that habit. You are laying the groundwork for future habits. Some breeders find that soft music can soothe a crying pup and help him get to sleep.

**SOCIALIZING YOUR PUPPY**
The first 20 weeks of your Scottish Deerhound puppy's life are the most important of his entire lifetime. A properly socialized puppy will grow up to be a confident and stable adult who will be a pleasure to live with and a welcome addition to the neighborhood.

The importance of socialization cannot be overemphasized. Research on canine behavior has proven that puppies who are not exposed to new sights, sounds, people and animals during their first 20 weeks of life will grow up to be timid and fearful, even aggressive, and unable to flourish outside of their home environment.

Socializing your puppy is not difficult and, in fact, will be a fun time for you both. Lead training

It's dinner for two for Lottie and litter brother Lucky, pictured at 11 weeks of age.

goes hand in hand with socialization, so your puppy will be learning how to walk on a lead at the same time that he's meeting the neighborhood. Because the Scottish Deerhound is such a terrific breed, everyone will enjoy meeting "the new kid on the block." Take him for short walks, to the park and to other dog-friendly places where he will encounter new people, especially children. Puppies automatically recognize children as "little people" and are drawn to play with them. Just make sure that you supervise these meetings and that the children do not get too rough or encourage him to play too hard. An overzealous pup can often nip too hard, frightening the child and in turn making the puppy overly excited. A bad experience in puppyhood can impact a dog for life, so a pup that has a negative experience with a child may grow up to be shy or even aggressive around children.

Take your puppy along on your daily errands. Puppies are natural "people magnets," and most people who see your pup will want to pet him. All of these encounters will help to mold him into a confident adult dog. Likewise, you will soon feel like a confident, responsible dog owner, rightly proud of your mannerly Scottish Deerhound.

Be especially careful of your puppy's encounters and experiences during the eight-to-ten-week-old period, which is also called the "fear period." This is a serious imprinting period, and all contact during this time should be gentle and positive. A frightening or negative event could leave a permanent impression that could affect his future behavior if a similar situation arises.

Also make sure that your puppy has received his first and second rounds of vaccinations before you expose him to other dogs or bring him to places that other dogs may frequent. Avoid dog parks and other strange-dog areas until your vet assures you that your puppy is fully immunized and resistant to the diseases that can be passed between canines. Discuss safe early socialization with your breeder and vet, as some recommend socializing the puppy even before he has received all of his inoculations.

## LEADER OF THE PUPPY'S PACK

Like other canines, your puppy needs an authority figure, someone he can look up to and regard as the leader of his "pack." His first pack leader was his dam, who taught him to be polite and not chew too hard on her ears or nip at her muzzle. He learned those same lessons from his littermates. If he played too rough, they cried in pain and stopped the game, which sent an important message to the rowdy puppy.

As puppies play together, they are also struggling to determine who will be the boss. Being pack animals, dogs need someone to be in charge. If a litter of puppies remained together beyond puppyhood, one of the pups would emerge as the strongest one, the one who calls the shots.

Once your puppy leaves the pack, he will look intuitively for a new leader. If he does not recognize you as that leader, he will try to assume that position for himself. Of course, it is hard to imagine your adorable Scottish Deerhound puppy trying to be in

### THE FAMILY FELINE

A resident cat has feline squatter's rights. The cat will treat the newcomer (your puppy) as she sees fit, regardless of what you do or say. So it's best to let the two of them work things out on their own terms. Cats have a height advantage and will generally leap to higher ground to avoid direct contact with a rambunctious pup. Some will hiss and boldly swat at a pup who passes by or tries to reach the cat. Keep the puppy under control in the presence of the cat to help them become accustomed to each other.

Deerhound owners must realize the breed's propensity to chase small animals like cats. For a better chance at harmonious living, the Deerhound pup should be raised with cats rather than being introduced to felines after he's become an adult.

charge when he is still so small and seemingly helpless. You must remember that these are natural canine instincts. Do not cave in and allow your pup to get the upper "paw"!

Just as socialization is so important during these first 20 weeks, so too is your puppy's early education. He was born without any bad habits. He does not know what is good or bad behavior. If he does things like nipping and digging, it's because he is having fun and doesn't know that humans consider these things as "bad." It's your job to teach him proper puppy manners, and this is the best time to accomplish that...before he has developed bad habits, since it is much more difficult to "unlearn" or correct unacceptable learned behavior than to teach good behavior from the start.

Make sure that all members of the family understand the importance of being consistent when training their new puppy. If you tell the puppy to stay off the sofa and your daughter allows him to cuddle on the couch to watch her favorite television show, your pup will be confused about what he is and is not allowed to do. Have a family conference before your pup comes home so that everyone understands the basic principles of puppy training and the rules you have set forth for the pup, and agrees to follow them.

The old saying that "an ounce of prevention is worth a pound of cure" is especially true when it comes to puppies. It is much easier to prevent inappropriate behavior than it is to change it. It's also easier and less stressful for the pup, since it will keep discipline to a minimum and create a more positive learning environment for him. That, in turn, will also be easier on you.

## SOLVING PUPPY PROBLEMS

### PUPPY WHINING

Puppies often cry and whine, just as infants and little children do. It's their way of telling us that they are lonely or in need of attention. Your puppy will miss his littermates and will feel insecure when he is left alone. You may be out of the house or just in another room, but he will still feel alone. During these times, the puppy's crate should be his personal comfort station, a place all his own where he can feel safe and secure. Once he learns that being alone is okay and not something to be feared, he will settle down without crying or objecting. You might want to leave a radio on while he is crated, as the sound of human voices can be soothing and will give the impression that people are around.

Give your puppy a favorite cuddly toy or chew toy to entertain him whenever he is crated. You will both be happier: the puppy because he is safe in his den and you because he is quiet, safe and not getting into puppy escapades that can wreak havoc in your house or cause him danger.

To make sure that your puppy will always view his crate as a safe and cozy place, never, ever, use the crate as punishment. That's the best way to turn the crate into a negative place that the pup will want to avoid. Sure, you can use the crate for your own peace of mind if your puppy is getting into trouble and needs some "time out." Just don't let him know that! Never scold the pup and immediately place him into the crate. Count to ten, give him a couple of hugs and maybe a treat, then scoot him into his crate.

It's also important not to make a big fuss when he is released from the crate. That will make getting out of the crate more appealing than being in the crate, which is just the opposite of what you are trying to achieve.

At 11 weeks of age, puppy Lottie towers over her adult Dachshund friend.

**REPEAT YOURSELF**

Puppies learn best through repetition. Use the same verbal cues and commands when teaching your puppy new behaviors or correcting for misbehaviors. Be consistent, but not monotonous. Puppies get bored just like puppy owners.

## "COUNTER SURFING"

What we like to call "counter surfing" usually starts to happen as soon as a puppy realizes that he is big enough to stand on his hind legs and investigate the good stuff on the kitchen counter or the coffee table. Once again, you have to be there to prevent it! As soon as you see your Scottish Deerhound even start to raise himself up, startle him with a sharp "No!" or "Aaahh, aaahh!" If he succeeds and manages to get one or both paws on the forbidden surface, smack those paws gently and firmly tell him "Off!" As soon as he's back on all four paws, command him to sit and praise at once.

For surf prevention, make sure to keep any tempting treats or edibles well out of reach, where your Scottish Deerhound can't see or smell them. It's the old rule of prevention yet again.

# SCOTTISH DEERHOUND

## SPECIAL FEEDING CONSIDERATIONS

Your Scottish Deerhound will appreciate being fed at regular times, and initially you should be guided by the breeder as to what type of food should be fed and when. When you buy your puppy, the breeder should provide you with a diet sheet, giving full details. If you have reason to alter the diet, you will be at liberty to change that food as the youngster matures, but any changes should be made gradually.

Knowing what diet works best for dogs of his line, every Scottish Deerhound breeder has his own personal preferences regarding the diet for his hounds. Regardless of type of food, it is wiser and healthier for the dog's digestion to give a Deerhound two, or even three, smaller meals each day, rather than just one.

At one time many owners fed fresh meat, but with so many good complete canine foods now available, this is no longer necessary. However, there is never any harm in adding a few cooked diced vegetables to your hound's meal to add a little variety. Always remember that a Scottish Deerhound is a large dog with a large appetite.

Owners who choose to feed fresh meat should vary the diet by feeding white meat or fish once or twice a week, as too much red meat can overheat the blood. Whichever diet you choose, it should be carefully balanced and

### FEEDING IN HOT WEATHER

Even the most dedicated chow hound may have less of an appetite when the weather is hot or humid. If your dog leaves more of his food behind than usual, adjust his portions until the weather and his appetite return to normal. Never leave the uneaten portion in the bowl, hoping he will return to finish it, because higher temperatures encourage food spoilage and bacterial growth.

should never be too high in protein. Scottish Deerhounds that are coursed, though, can cope with a slightly higher protein content.

Because Scottish Deerhounds are deep-chested dogs, special daily precautions related to your dog's feeding and exercise must be implemented to protect him from the deadly bloat (gastric torsion). For example, it is of great importance that your Scottish Deerhound is not fed for at least an hour after exercise and is not exercised for at least an hour after feeding, although he may be allowed outside briefly to relieve himself if needed. Feeding too close to exercise can have a deadly effect. After a particularly hectic day, such as at a coursing meeting or a show, your Scottish Deerhound should be given plenty of time to settle down before food is offered. Always ensure that plenty of water is available in between meals, although never allow him to gulp water.

**FEEDING THE PUPPY**
Of course, your pup's very first food will be his dam's milk. There may be special situations in which pups fail to nurse, necessitating that the breeder hand-feed them with a formula, but for the most part pups spend the first weeks of life nursing from their dam. The breeder weans the pups by gradually introducing solid foods and decreasing the milk meals. Pups may even start themselves off on the weaning process, albeit inadvertently, if they snatch bites from their mom's food bowl.

By the time the pups are ready for new homes, they are fully weaned and eating a good puppy food. As a new owner, you

may be thinking, "Great! The breeder has taken care of the hard part." Not so fast.

A puppy's first year of life is the time when most of his growth and development takes place. This is a delicate time, especially for a large-breed pup, and diet plays a huge role in proper skeletal and muscular formation. Improper diet and exercise habits can lead to damaging problems that will compromise the dog's health and movement for his entire life. That being said, new owners should not worry needlessly. With the myriad types of food formulated specifically for growing pups of different-sized

**NOT HUNGRY?**
No dog in his right mind would turn down his dinner, would he? If you notice that your dog has lost interest in his food, there could be any number of causes. Dental problems are a common cause of appetite loss, one that is often overlooked. If your dog has a toothache, a loose tooth or sore gums from infection, chances are it doesn't feel so good to chew. Think about when you've had a toothache! If your dog does not approach the food bowl with his usual enthusiasm, look inside his mouth for signs of a problem. Whatever the cause, you'll want to consult your vet so that your chow hound can get back to his happy, hungry self as soon as possible.

breeds, dog-food manufacturers have taken much of the guesswork out of feeding your puppy well. Since growth-food formulas are designed to provide the nutrition that a growing puppy needs, it is unnecessary and, in fact, can prove harmful to add supplements to the diet. Research has shown that too much of certain vitamin supplements and minerals predispose a dog to skeletal problems. It's by no means a case of "if a little is good, a lot is better." At every stage of your dog's life, too much or too little in the way of nutrients can be harmful, which is why a manufactured complete food is the easiest way to know that your dog is getting what he needs.

Because of a young pup's small body and accordingly small digestive system, his daily portion will be divided up into small meals throughout the day. This can mean starting off with three or more meals a day and decreasing the number of meals as the pup matures to the adult feeding schedule of two meals on a morning/evening schedule. Your Scottish Deerhound can be switched to an adult-formula food around ten months of age.

Regarding the feeding schedule, feeding the pup at the same times and in the same place each

The breeder will have started the pups on a quality puppy food and should provide you with a diet sheet so that you can continue feeding a proper diet.

day is important for both house-breaking purposes and establishing the dog's everyday routine. As for the amount to feed, growing puppies generally need proportionately more food per body weight than their adult counterparts, but a pup should never be allowed to gain excess weight. Dogs of all ages should be kept in proper body condition, but extra weight can strain a pup's developing frame, causing skeletal problems.

Watch your pup's weight as he grows and, if the recommended amounts seem to be too much or too little for your pup, consult the vet about appropriate dietary changes. Keep in mind that treats, although small, can quickly add up throughout the day, contributing unnecessary calories. Treats are fine when used prudently; opt for dog treats specially formulated to be healthy or for nutritious snacks like small pieces of cheese or cooked chicken.

**FEEDING THE ADULT DOG**
For the adult (meaning physically mature) dog, feeding properly is about maintenance, not growth. Again, correct weight is a concern. Your dog should appear fit and should have an evident "waist." His ribs should not be protruding (a sign of being underweight), but they should be covered by only a slight layer of fat. Under normal circumstances,

an adult dog can be maintained fairly easily with a high-quality nutritionally complete adult-formula food.

Factor treats into your dog's overall daily caloric intake and avoid offering table scraps. Not only are certain "people foods," like chocolate, onions, grapes, raisins and nuts, toxic to dogs but feeding from the table also encourages begging and overeating. Overweight dogs are more prone to health problems. Research has even shown that obesity takes years off a dog's life. With that in mind, resist the urge to overfeed and over-treat. Don't make unnecessary additions to your dog's diet, whether with tidbits or with extra vitamins and minerals.

The amount of food needed for proper maintenance will vary depending on the individual dog's activity level, but you will be able to tell whether the daily portions are keeping him in good shape. It's been shown that an adult Deerhound's food should not have too high of a protein content, although coursing dogs can have a bit more protein than pets or show dogs. With the wide variety of good complete foods available, choosing what to feed is largely a matter of personal preference. Just as with the puppy, the adult dog should have consistency in his mealtimes and feeding place. In addition to a consistent routine, regular mealtimes also allow the owner to incorporate the necessary daily bloat precautions and to see how much his dog is eating. If the dog seems never to be satisfied or, likewise, becomes uninterested in his food, the owner will know right away that something is wrong and can consult the vet.

**DIETS FOR THE AGING DOG**
Based on his large size, a Scottish Deerhound will reach "senior citizen" status at about six or seven years of age. In general, smaller breeds live longer than larger ones.

What does aging have to do with your dog's diet? No, he won't get a discount at the local diner's early-bird special. Yes, he will require some dietary changes to accommodate the changes that come along with increased age. Many Scottish Deerhound owners

*Be sure to purchase bowls large enough to hold a Deerhound's portions.*

simply reduce food portions rather than switching to a different type of food. Nonetheless, discuss with your vet whether you need to switch to a higher-protein or senior-formulated food or whether your current adult-dog food contains sufficient nutrition for the senior.

Watching the dog's weight remains essential, even more so in the senior stage. Older dogs are already more vulnerable to illness, and obesity only contributes to their susceptibility to problems. As the older dog becomes less active and, thus, exercises less, his regular portions may cause him to gain weight. At this point, you may consider decreasing his daily food intake or switching to a reduced-calorie food. As with all changes, you should consult your vet for advice.

**DON'T FORGET THE WATER!**
There's no doubt that your Deerhound needs plenty of water. Fresh cold water, in a clean bowl, should be available to your dog at all times except mealtimes for bloat prevention. There are also special circumstances, such as during puppy housebreaking, when you will want to monitor your pup's water intake so that you will be able to predict when he will need to relieve himself, but water must be available to him nonetheless. Water is essential for hydration

# WHAT IS "BLOAT"?

Need yet another reason to avoid tossing your dog a morsel from your plate? It is shown that dogs fed table scraps have an increased risk of developing bloat, or gastric torsion. Did you know that more occurrences of bloat occur in the warm-weather months due to the frequency of outdoor cooking and dining and dogs' receiving "samples" from the fired-up grill?

You likely have heard the term "bloat," which refers to gastric torsion (gastric dilatation/volvulus), a potentially fatal condition. As it is directly related to feeding and exercise practices, a brief explanation here is warranted. The term *dilatation* means that the dog's stomach is filled with air, while *volvulus* means that the stomach is twisted around on itself, blocking the entrance/exit points. Dilatation/volvulus is truly a deadly combination, although they also can occur independently of each other. An affected dog cannot digest food or pass gas, and blood cannot flow to the stomach, causing accumulation of toxins and gas, great pain and shock.

Many theories exist on what exactly causes bloat, but we do know that deep-chested breeds are more prone. Activities like eating a large meal, gulping water, strenuous exercise too close to mealtimes, stress, overexcitement or a combination of these factors can contribute to bloat, though not every case is directly related to these more well-known causes. With that in mind, we can focus on incorporating simple daily preventives and knowing how to recognize the symptoms; ask your vet about both. Affected dogs need immediate veterinary attention, as death can result quickly. Signs include obvious restlessness/discomfort, crying in pain, drooling/excessive salivation, unproductive attempts to vomit or relieve himself, visibly bloated appearance and collapsing. Do not wait: get to a vet right away if you see any of these symptoms. The vet will confirm by x-ray if the stomach is bloated with air; if so, the dog must be treated *immediately*.

A bloated dog will be treated for shock, and the stomach must be relieved of the air pressure as well as surgically returned to its correct position. If part of the stomach wall has died, that part must be removed. Usually the stomach is stapled to the abdominal wall to prevent another episode of bloating; this may or may not be successful. The vet should also check the dog for heart problems resulting from the condition.

**EXERCISE ALERT!**
You should be careful where you exercise your dog. Many countryside areas have been sprayed with chemicals that are highly toxic to both dogs and humans. Never allow your dog to eat grass or drink from puddles on either public or private grounds, as the run-off water may contain chemicals from sprays and herbicides.

and proper body function just as it is in humans.

You will get to know how much your dog typically drinks in a day. Of course, in the heat or if exercising vigorously, he will be more thirsty and will drink more. However, if he begins to drink noticeably more water for no apparent reason, this could signal any of various problems, and you are advised to consult your vet.

Water is the best drink for dogs. Some owners are tempted to give milk from time to time or to moisten dry food with milk, but dogs do not have the enzymes necessary to digest the lactose in milk, which is much different from the milk that nursing puppies receive. Therefore stick with clean fresh water to quench your dog's thirst.

A word of caution concerning your deep-chested dog's water intake: he should never be allowed to gulp water, especially at mealtimes. In fact, his water intake should be avoided at mealtimes as a rule. This simple daily precaution can go a long way in protecting your dog from the dangerous and potentially fatal gastric torsion (bloat).

**EXERCISE**
Adult Scottish Deerhounds certainly need regular exercise, and this must be very seriously considered before adding a Deerhound to your life. It is said that Scottish Deerhounds will readily accept as much exercise as their owners can give them, and this is very true. One should also bear in mind that, although generally well behaved, adult Scottish Deerhounds are very strong and must be trained to walk politely on a lead and not to pull.

However, with regard to youngsters, it is important not to over-exercise a Scottish Deerhound puppy, particularly not while his bones are still growing. A puppy should have no more than 20 minutes of on-lead walking each day, and although he will also require free exercise, this should be restricted to a limited (and of course enclosed) space. In a youngster, exercise should be built up slowly.

To keep their limbs and muscles in fit condition, Scottish Deerhounds should be exercised on a combination of surfaces. Lead work should be done, at least in part, on a hard surface, such as sidewalks or pavement. Coupled with this, free exercise is needed on softer ground such as an enclosed grassy area. Along with keeping feeding and exercise times at least an hour apart, always make sure your Deerhound can rest after exercise in a comfortable temperature.

## GROOMING

Scottish Deerhounds are rarely, if ever, bathed, but a certain amount of "tidying up" is done to the coat. However, one must always remember that this is a rough-coated breed and, as such, the coat is shaggy. Different people choose to tidy their hounds' coats to a greater or lesser extent, but this is not a breed that should end up looking "sculptured" in any way. The coat of the Scottish Deerhound does not shed very much, but it does tangle somewhat, so an occasional comb-

through with a wide-toothed comb is needed.

The coat on the ears should be like that of a mouse, and to emphasize the appearance of neatness and smallness of the ear, long hairs are usually removed, especially on show dogs. Another area that sometimes needs attention is the foot, as it must look compact. Any hairs detracting from the shape of the foot should be carefully tidied.

The puppy is introduced to grooming at a young age. This grooming tool has a bristle brush on one side and a pin brush on the other.

A thorough once-over on a regular basis will remove any mats, tangles and debris. This Deerhound is being brushed with a pin brush.

bath when he is young, he will become accustomed to the process. Wrestling a dog into the tub or chasing a freshly shampooed dog who has escaped from the bath will be no fun! Most dogs don't naturally enjoy their baths, but you at least want yours to cooperate with you.

Before bathing the dog, have the items you'll need close at hand. First, decide where you will bathe the dog. You should have a tub or basin with a non-slip surface. In warm weather, some like to use a portable pool in the yard, although you'll want to make sure that your dog doesn't head for the nearest dirt pile following his bath! You will also need a hose or shower spray to wet the coat thoroughly, a shampoo formulated for dogs and absorbent towels. Human shampoos are too harsh for dogs' coats and will dry them out.

Before wetting the dog, give him a brush-through to remove any dead hair, dirt and mats. Make sure he is at ease in the tub and have the water at a comfortable temperature. Begin bathing by wetting the coat all the way down to the skin. Massage in the shampoo, keeping it away from his face and eyes. Rinse him thoroughly, again avoiding the eyes and ears, as you don't want to get water into the ear canals. A thorough rinsing is important, as shampoo residue is drying and itchy to the dog. After rinsing,

## BATHING

In general, Scottish Deerhounds are bathed rarely, possibly only if your dog gets into something messy or if he starts to smell like a dog. Show dogs are usually bathed before every show, which could be as frequent as weekly, although this depends on the owner. Bathing too frequently can have negative effects on the skin and coat, removing natural oils and causing dryness.

If you give your dog his first

wrap him in a towel to absorb the initial moisture. You can finish drying with another towel or a blow dryer on low heat, held at a safe distance from the dog. You should keep the dog indoors and away from drafts until he is completely dry.

## NAIL CLIPPING

Having his nails trimmed is not on many dogs' lists of favorite things to do but is very important for Deerhounds. The feet of a Scottish Deerhound are to be well knuckled, and long nails will cause the toes to splay out. With this in mind, you will need to accustom your puppy to the procedure at a young age so that he will sit still (well, as still as he can) for his pedicures. Long nails can cause the dog's feet to spread, which is not good for him; likewise, long nails can hurt if they unintentionally scratch, not good for you!

Some dogs' nails are worn down naturally by regular walking on hard surfaces, so the frequency with which you clip depends on your individual dog. Look at his nails from time to time and clip as needed; a good way to know when it's time for a trim is if you hear your dog clicking as he walks across the floor.

There are several types of nail clippers and even electric nail-grinding tools made for dogs; first we'll discuss using the clipper. To start, have your clipper ready and some doggie treats on hand. You want your pup to view his nail-clipping sessions in a positive light, and what better way to convince him than with food? You may want to enlist the help of an assistant to comfort the pup and offer treats as you concentrate on the clipping itself. A Scottish Deerhound's nails are strong, so this can make them difficult to trim without the right equipment. For Scottish Deerhounds, I have found that canine nail clippers of the guillotine type are far more efficient than those with straight edges. The nail tip is inserted into the opening, and

A wide-toothed metal comb is helpful for detangling the Deerhound's rough coat.

blades on the top and bottom snip it off in one clip.

Start by grasping the pup's paw; a little pressure on the foot pad causes the nail to extend, making it easier to clip. Clip off a little at a time. If you can see the "quick," which is a blood vessel that runs through each nail, you will know how much to trim, as you do not want to cut into the quick. On that note, if you do cut the quick, which will cause bleeding, you can stem the flow of blood with a styptic pencil or other clotting agent; in an emergency, household flour is said to help stem the bloodflow from a nail. If you mistakenly nip the quick, do not panic or fuss, as this will cause the pup to be afraid. Simply reassure the pup, stop the bleeding and move on to the next nail. Don't be discouraged; you will become a professional canine pedicurist with practice.

You may or may not be able to see the quick, so it's best to just clip off a small bit at a time. If you see a dark dot in the center of the nail, this is the quick and your cue to stop clipping. Tell the puppy he's a "good boy" and offer a piece of treat with each nail. You can also use nail-clipping time to examine the footpads, making sure that they are not dry and cracked and that nothing has become embedded in them.

The nail grinder, the other choice, is preferred by some owners. Accustoming the puppy to the sound of the grinder is relatively easy, and there's no chance of cutting through the quick. Use the grinder on a low setting and always talk soothingly to your dog. He won't mind his salon visit, and he'll have nicely polished nails as well. Just be sure not to get the grinder caught in the coat!

### Ear Cleaning

While keeping your dog's ears clean unfortunately will not cause him to "hear" your commands any better, it will protect him from ear infection and ear-mite infestation. In addition, a dog's ears are vulnerable to waxy build-up and to collecting foreign matter from the outdoors. Look in your dog's ears regularly to ensure that they look pink, clean and otherwise healthy. Even if they look fine, an odor in the ears signals a problem and means it's time to call the vet.

A dog's ears should be cleaned regularly; once a week is suggested, and you can do this along with your regular brushing. Using a cotton ball or pad, and never probing into the ear canal, wipe the ear gently. You can use an ear-cleansing liquid or powder available from your vet or pet-supply store; alternatively, you might prefer to use homemade solutions with ingredients like one part white vinegar and one part hydrogen peroxide. Ask your vet about home remedies before you attempt to concoct something on your own!

Keep your dog's ears free of excess hair by plucking it as needed. If done gently, this will be painless for the dog. Look for wax, brown droppings (a sign of ear mites), redness or any other abnormalities. At the first sign of a problem, contact your vet so that he can prescribe an appropriate medication.

### EYE CARE

During grooming sessions, pay extra attention to the condition of your dog's eyes. If the area around the eyes is soiled or if tear staining has occurred, there are various cleaning agents made especially for this purpose. Look at the dog's eyes to make sure no debris has entered; dogs with large eyes and those who spend time outdoors are especially prone to this.

> ### SCOOTING HIS BOTTOM
> Here's a doggy problem that many owners tend to neglect. If your dog is scooting his rear end around the carpet, he probably is experiencing anal-sac impaction or blockage. The anal sacs are the two grape-sized glands on either side of the dog's vent. The dog cannot empty these glands, which become filled with a foul-smelling material. The dog may attempt to lick the area to relieve the pressure. He may also rub his anus on your walls, furniture or floors.
>
> Don't neglect your dog's rear end during grooming sessions. By squeezing both sides of the anus with a soft cloth, you can express some of the material in the sacs. If the material is pasty and thick, you likely will need the assistance of a veterinarian. Vets know how to express the glands and can show you how to do it correctly without hurting the dog or spraying yourself with the unpleasant liquid.

The signs of an eye infection are obvious: mucus, redness, puffiness, scabs or other signs of irritation. If your dog's eyes become infected, the vet will likely prescribe an antibiotic ointment for treatment. If you notice signs of more serious problems, such as opacities in the eye, which usually indicate cataracts, consult the vet at once. Taking time to pay attention to your dog's eyes will alert you in the early stages of any problem so that you can get your dog treatment as soon as possible. You could save your dog's sight!

**ID FOR YOUR DOG**
You love your Scottish Deerhound and want to keep him safe. Of course you take every precaution to prevent his escaping from the yard or becoming lost or stolen. You have a sturdy high fence and you always keep your dog on lead when out and about in public places. If your dog is not properly identified, however, you are overlooking a major aspect of his safety. We hope to never be in a situation where our dog is missing, but we should practice prevention in the unfortunate case that this happens; identification greatly increases the chances of your dog's being returned to you.

There are several ways to identify your dog. First, the traditional dog tag should be a staple in your dog's wardrobe, attached to his everyday collar. Tags can be made of sturdy plastic and various metals and should include your contact information so that a person who finds the dog can get in touch with you right away to arrange his return. Many people today enjoy the wide range of decorative tags available, so have fun and create a tag to match your dog's personality. Of course, it is important that the tag stays on the collar, so have a secure "O" ring

**PET OR STRAY?**
Besides the obvious benefit of providing your contact information to whoever finds your lost dog, an ID tag makes your dog more approachable and more likely to be recovered. A strange dog wandering the neighborhood without a collar and tags will look like a stray, while the collar and tags indicate that the dog is someone's pet. Even if the ID tags become detached from the collar, the collar alone will make a person more likely to pick up the dog.

attachment; you also can explore the type of tag that slides right onto the collar.

In addition to the ID tag, which every dog should wear even if identified by another method, two other forms of identification have become popular: microchipping and tattooing. In microchipping, a tiny scannable chip is painlessly inserted under the dog's skin. The number is registered to you so that, if your lost dog turns up at a clinic or shelter, the chip can be scanned to retrieve your contact information.

The advantage of the microchip is that it is a permanent form of ID, but there are some factors to consider. Several different companies make microchips, and not all are compatible with the others' scanning devices. It's best to find a company with a universal microchip that can be read by scanners made by other companies as well. It won't do any good to have the dog chipped if the information cannot be retrieved. Also, not every humane society, shelter and clinic is equipped with a scanner, although more and more facilities are equipping themselves. In fact, many shelters microchip dogs that they adopt out to new homes.

In the US, there are five or six major microchip manufacturers as well as a few databases. The American Kennel Club's Companion Animal Recovery unit works in conjunction with HomeAgain™ Companion Animal Retrieval System (Schering-Plough). In the UK, The Kennel Club is affiliated with the National Pet Register, operated by Wood Green Animal Shelters.

Because the microchip is not visible to the eye, the dog must wear a tag that states that he is microchipped so that whoever picks him up will know to have him scanned. The tag also lists the registry's phone number and the dog's microchip number. Your dog of course also should have a tag with your contact information in case his microchip information cannot be retrieved. Humane societies and veterinary clinics offer microchipping service, which is usually very affordable.

Though less popular than microchipping, tattooing is another permanent method of ID for dogs.

Most vets perform this service, and there are also clinics that perform dog tattooing. This is also an affordable procedure and one that will not cause much discomfort for the dog. It is best to put the tattoo in a visible area, such as the ear, to deter theft. It is sad to say that there are cases of dogs' being stolen and sold to research laboratories, but such laboratories will not accept tattooed dogs.

To ensure that the tattoo is effective in aiding your dog's return to you, the tattoo number must be registered with a national organization. That way, when someone finds a tattooed dog, a phone call to the registry will quickly match the dog with his owner.

## CAR CAUTION

You may like to bring your canine companion along on the daily errands, but if you will be running in and out from place to place and can't bring him indoors with you, leave him at home. Your dog should never be left alone in the car, not even for a minute—never! A car heats up very quickly, and even a cracked-open window will not help. In fact, leaving the window cracked will be dangerous if the dog becomes uncomfortable and tries to escape. A dog in a car also can be a target for dog thieves. When in doubt, leave your dog home, where you know he will be safe.

# SCOTTISH DEERHOUND

**BASIC TRAINING PRINCIPLES: PUPPY VS. ADULT**

There's a big difference between training an adult dog and training a young puppy. With a young puppy, everything is new. At eight to ten weeks of age, he will be experiencing many things, and he has nothing with which to compare these experiences. Up to this point, he has been with his dam and littermates, not one-on-one with people except in his

*Proper training ensures that you and your Deerhound will see eye to eye!*

interactions with his breeder and visitors to the litter.

When you first bring the puppy home, he is eager to please you. This means that he accepts doing things your way. During the next couple of months, he will absorb the basis of everything he needs to know for the rest of his life. This early age is even referred to as the "sponge" stage. After that, for the next 18 months, it's up to you to reinforce good manners by building on the foundation that you've established. Once your puppy is reliable in basic commands and behavior and has reached the appropriate age, you may gradually introduce him to some of the interesting sports, games and activities available to pet owners and their dogs.

Raising your puppy is a family affair. Each member of the family must know what rules to set forth for the puppy and how to use the same one-word commands to mean exactly the same thing every time. Even if yours is a large family, one person will soon be considered by the pup to be the leader, the alpha person in his pack, the "boss" who must be

## BASIC PRINCIPLES OF DOG TRAINING

1. Start training early. A young puppy is ready, willing and able.
2. Timing is your all-important tool. Praise at the exact time that the dog responds correctly. Pay close attention.
3. Patience is almost as important as timing!
4. Repeat! The same word has to mean the same thing every time.
5. In the beginning, praise all correct behavior verbally, along with treats and petting.

Life with a well-trained Scottish Deerhound is mutually rewarding.

obeyed. Often that highly regarded person turns out to be the one who feeds the puppy. Food ranks very high on the puppy's list of important things! That's why your puppy is rewarded with small treats along with verbal praise when he responds to you correctly. As the puppy learns to do what you want him to do, the food rewards are gradually eliminated and only the praise remains. If you were to keep up with the food treats, you could have two problems on your hands—an obese dog and a beggar.

Training begins the minute your Scottish Deerhound puppy steps through the doorway of your home, so don't make the mistake of putting the puppy on the floor and telling him by your actions to "Go for it! Run wild!" Even if this is your first puppy, you must act as

if you know what you're doing: be the boss. An uncertain pup may be terrified to move, while a bold one will be ready to take you at your word and start plotting to destroy the house! Before you collected your puppy, you decided where his own special place would be, and that's where to put him when you first arrive home. Give him a house tour after he has investigated his area and had a nap and a bathroom "pit stop."

It's worth mentioning here that, if you've adopted an adult dog that is completely trained to your liking, lucky you! You're off the hook! However, if that dog spent his life up to this point in a kennel, or even in a good home but without any real training, be prepared to tackle the job ahead. A dog three years of age or older with no previous training cannot

**BE UPSTANDING!**
You are the dog's leader. During training, stand up straight so your dog looks up at you, and therefore up *to* you. Say the command words distinctly, in a clear, declarative tone of voice. (No barking!) Give rewards only as the correct response takes place (remember your timing!). Praise, smiles and treats are "rewards" used to positively reinforce correct responses. Don't repeat a mistake. Just change to another exercise—you will soon find success!

be blamed for not knowing what he was never taught. While the dog is trying to understand and

learn your rules, at the same time he has to unlearn many of his previously self-taught habits and general view of the world.

Working with a professional trainer will speed up your progress with an adopted adult dog. You'll need patience, too. Some new rules may be close to impossible for the dog to accept. After all, he's been successful so far by doing everything his way! (Patience again.) He may agree with your instruction for a few days and then slip back into his old ways, so you must be just as consistent and understanding in your teaching as you would be with a puppy. (More patience needed yet again!) Your dog has to learn to pay attention to your voice, your family, the daily routine, new smells, new sounds and, in some cases, even a new climate.

One of the most important things to find out about a newly adopted adult dog is his reaction to children (yours and others), strangers and your friends, and how he acts upon meeting other dogs. If he was not socialized with dogs as a puppy, this could be a major problem. This does not mean that he's a "bad" dog, a vicious dog or an aggressive dog; rather, it means that he has no idea how to read another dog's body language. There's no way for him to tell whether the other dog is a friend or foe. Survival instinct takes over, telling him to attack first and ask questions later. This definitely calls for professional help and, even then, may not be a behavior that can be corrected 100% reliably (or even at all). If you have a puppy, this is why it is so very important to introduce your young puppy properly to other puppies and "dog-friendly" adult dogs.

## HOUSE-TRAINING YOUR SCOTTISH DEERHOUND

Dogs are tactility-oriented when it comes to house-training. In other words, they respond to the surface on which they are given approval to eliminate. The choice is yours (the dog's version is in parentheses): The lawn (including the neighbors' lawns)? A bare patch of earth under a tree (where people like to sit and relax in the summertime)? Concrete steps or patio (all sidewalks, garages and basement floors)? The curbside (watch out for cars)? A small area of crushed stone in a corner of the yard (mine!)? The latter is the best choice if you can manage it because it will remain strictly for the dog's use and is easy to keep clean.

You can start out with paper-training indoors and switch over to an outdoor surface as the puppy matures and gains control over his need to eliminate. For the nay-sayers, don't worry—this won't mean that the dog will soil on every piece of newspaper lying around the house. You are training him to go outside, remember? Starting out by paper-training often is the only choice for a city dog.

### WHEN YOUR PUPPY'S "GOT TO GO"

Your puppy's need to relieve himself is seemingly non-stop, but signs of improvement will be seen each week. From 8 to 10 weeks old, the puppy will have to be taken outside every time he wakes up, about 10–15 minutes after every meal and after every period of play—all day long, from first thing in the morning until his bedtime! That's a total of ten or more trips per day to teach the puppy where it's okay to relieve himself. With that schedule in mind, you can see that house-training a young puppy is not a part-time job. It requires someone to be home all day.

If that seems overwhelming or impossible, do a little planning.

Your puppy looks up to you for love, care, safety, guidance and discipline.

Young puppies naturally stay close to their owners and will follow them from place to place, but puppies grow curious and tend to explore, which is why teaching the dog to come to you is so important.

For example, plan to pick up your puppy at the start of a vacation period. If you can't get home in the middle of the day, plan to hire a dog-sitter or ask a neighbor to come over to take the pup outside, feed him his lunch and then take him out again about ten or so minutes after he's eaten. Also make arrangements with that or another person to be your "emergency" contact if you have to stay late on the job. Remind yourself—repeatedly—that this hectic schedule improves as the puppy gets older.

### HOME WITHIN A HOME

Your Scottish Deerhound puppy needs to be confined to one secure, puppy-proof area when no one is able to watch his every move. Generally, the kitchen is the place of choice because the floor is washable. Likewise, it's a busy family area that will accustom the pup to a variety of noises, everything from pots and pans to the telephone, blender and dishwasher. He will also be enchanted by the smell of your cooking (and will never be critical when you burn something). An exercise pen (also called an "ex-pen," a puppy version of a playpen) within the room of choice is an excellent means of confinement for a young pup. He can see out and has a certain amount of space in which to run about, but he is safe from dangerous things like electrical cords, heating units, trash baskets or open kitchen-supply cabinets. Place the pen where the puppy

### DAILY SCHEDULE

How many relief trips does your puppy need per day? A puppy up to the age of 14 weeks will need to go outside about 8 to 12 times per day! You will have to take the pup out any time he starts sniffing around the floor or turning in small circles, as well as after naps, meals, games and lessons or whenever he's released from his crate. Once the puppy is 14 to 22 weeks of age, he will require only 6 to 8 relief trips. At the ages of 22 to 32 weeks, the puppy will require about 5 to 7 trips. Adult dogs typically require 4 relief trips per day, in the morning, afternoon, evening and late at night.

will not get a blast of heat or air conditioning.

In the pen, you can put a few toys, his bed (which can be his crate if the dimensions of pen and crate are compatible) and a few layers of newspaper in one small corner, just in case. A water bowl can be hung at a convenient height on the side of the ex-pen so it won't become a splashing pool for an innovative puppy. His food dish can go on the floor, near but not under the water bowl.

Can you imagine handling a dog as large as a Scottish Deerhound—much less two—if he is not properly trained?

### LEASH TRAINING

House-training and leash training go hand in hand, literally. When taking your puppy outside to do his business, lead him there on his leash. Unless an emergency potty run is called for, do not whisk the puppy up into your arms and take him outside. If you have a fenced yard, you have the advantage of letting the puppy loose to go out, but it's better to put the dog on the leash and take him to his designated place in the yard until he is reliably house-trained. Taking the puppy for a walk is the best way to house-train a dog. The dog will associate the walk with his time to relieve himself, and the exercise of walking stimulates the dog's bowels and bladder. Dogs that are not trained to relieve themselves on a walk may hold it until they get back home, which of course defeats half the purpose of the walk.

Crates are something that pet owners are at last getting used to for their dogs. Wild or domestic canines have always preferred to sleep in den-like safe spots, and that is exactly what the crate provides. How often have you seen adult dogs that choose to sleep under a table or chair even though they have full run of the house? It's the den connection.

In your "happy" voice, use the word "Crate" every time you put the pup into his den. If he's new to a crate, toss in a small biscuit for him to chase the first few times. At night, after he's been outside, he should sleep in his crate. The crate may be kept in his designated area at night or, if you want to be sure to hear those wake-up yips in the morning, put the crate in a corner of your bedroom. However, don't

> **EXTRA! EXTRA!**
> The headlines read: "Puppy Piddles Here!" Breeders commonly use newspapers to line their whelping pens, so puppies learn to associate newspapers with relieving themselves. Do not use newspapers to line your pup's crate, as this will signal to your puppy that it is OK to urinate in his crate. If you choose to paper-train your puppy, you will layer newspapers on a section of the floor near the door he uses to go outside. You should encourage the puppy to use the papers to relieve himself, and bring him there whenever you see him getting ready to go. Little by little, you will reduce the size of the newspaper-covered area so that the puppy will learn to relieve himself "on the other side of the door."

make any response whatsoever to whining or crying. If he's completely ignored, he'll settle down and get to sleep.

Good bedding for a young puppy is an old folded bath towel or an old blanket, something that is easily washable and disposable if necessary ("accidents" will happen!). Never put newspaper in the puppy's crate. Also, those old ideas about adding a clock to replace his mother's heartbeat, or a hot-water bottle to replace her warmth, are just that—old ideas. The clock could drive the puppy nuts, and the hot-water bottle could end up as a very soggy waterbed! An extremely good breeder would have introduced your puppy to the crate by letting two pups sleep together for a couple of nights, followed by several nights alone. How thankful you will be if you found that breeder!

Safe toys in the pup's crate or area will keep him occupied, but monitor their condition closely. Discard any toys that show signs of being chewed to bits. Squeaky parts, bits of stuffing or plastic or any other small pieces can cause intestinal blockage or possibly choking if swallowed.

**PROGRESSING WITH POTTY-TRAINING**
After you've taken your puppy out and he has relieved himself in the area you've selected, he can have some free time with the

# Canine Development Schedule

It is important to understand how and at what age a puppy develops into adulthood. If you are a puppy owner, consult this Canine Development Schedule to determine the stage of development your puppy is currently experiencing. This knowledge will help you as you work with the puppy in the weeks and months ahead.

| Period | Age | Characteristics |
|---|---|---|
| First to Third | Birth to Seven Weeks | Puppy needs food, sleep and warmth and responds to simple and gentle touching. Needs mother for security and disciplining. Needs littermates for learning and interacting with other dogs. Pup learns to function within a pack and learns pack order of dominance. Begin socializing pup with adults and children for short periods. Pup begins to become aware of his environment. |
| Fourth | Eight to Twelve Weeks | Brain is fully developed. Pup needs socializing with outside world. Remove from mother and littermates. Needs to change from canine pack to human pack. Human dominance necessary. Fear period occurs between 8 and 12 weeks. Avoid fright and pain. |
| Fifth | Thirteen to Sixteen Weeks | Training and formal obedience should begin. Less association with other dogs, more with people, places, situations. Period will pass easily if you remember this is pup's change-to-adolescence time. Be firm and fair. Flight instinct prominent. Permissiveness and over-disciplining can do permanent damage. Praise for good behavior. |
| Juvenile | Four to Eight Months | Another fear period about seven to eight months of age. It passes quickly, but be cautious of fright and pain. Sexual maturity reached. Dominant traits established. Dog should understand sit, down, come and stay by now. |

Note: These are approximate time frames. Allow for individual differences in puppies.

family as long as there is someone responsible for watching him. That doesn't mean just someone in the same room who is watching TV or busy on the computer, but one person who is doing nothing other than keeping an eye on the pup, playing with him on the floor and helping him understand his position in the pack.

This first taste of freedom will let you begin to set the house rules. If you don't want the dog on the furniture, now is the time to prevent his first attempts to jump up onto the couch. The word to use in this case is "Off," not "Down." "Down" is the word you will use to teach the down position, which is something entirely different.

Most corrections at this stage come in the form of simply distracting the puppy. Instead of telling him "No" for "Don't chew the carpet," distract the chomping puppy with a toy and he'll forget about the carpet.

**Dogs respond best to structure. Establish a toileting schedule with your puppy and do your best to stick to it.**

As you are playing with the pup, do not forget to watch him closely and pay attention to his body language. Whenever you see him begin to circle or sniff, take the puppy outside to relieve himself. If you are paper-training, put him back into his confined area on the newspapers. In either case, praise him as he eliminates while he actually is *in the act* of relieving himself. Three seconds after he has finished is too late! You'll be praising him for running toward you, picking up a toy or whatever he may be doing at that moment, and that's not what you want to be praising him for. Timing is a vital tool in all dog training. Use it!

Remove soiled newspapers immediately and replace them with clean ones. You may want to take a small piece of soiled paper and place it in the middle of the new clean papers, as the scent will attract him to that spot when it's time to go again. That scent attraction is why it's so important to clean up any messes made in the house by using a product specially made to eliminate the odor of dog urine and droppings. Regular household cleansers won't do the trick. Pet shops sell the best pet deodorizers. Invest in the largest container you can find.

Scent attraction eventually will lead your pup to his chosen spot outdoors; this is the basis of outdoor training. When you take

## SOMEBODY TO BLAME

House-training a puppy can be frustrating for the puppy and the owner alike. The puppy does not instinctively understand the difference between defecating on the pavement outside and on the ceramic tile in the kitchen. He is confused and frightened by his human's exuberant reactions to his natural urges. The owner, arguably the more intelligent of the duo, is also frustrated that he cannot convince his puppy to obey his commands and instructions.

In frustration, the owner may struggle with the temptation to discipline the puppy, scold him or even strike him on the rear end. Harsh corrections are unnecessary and inappropriate, serving to defeat your purpose in gaining your puppy's trust and respect. Don't blame your nine-week-old puppy. Blame yourself for not being 100% consistent in the puppy's lessons and routine. The lesson here is simple: try harder and your puppy will succeed.

urinates and defecates. Move him a few feet in one direction or another if he's just sitting there looking at you, but remember that this is neither playtime nor time for a walk. This is strictly a business trip! Then, as he circles and squats (remember your timing!), give him a quiet "Good dog" as praise. If you start to jump for joy, ecstatic over his performance, he'll do one of two things: either he will stop mid-stream, as it were, or he'll do it again for you—in the house—and expect you to be just as delighted!

Give him five minutes or so and, if he doesn't go in that time, take him back indoors to his confined area and try again in another ten minutes, or immediately if you see him sniffing and circling. By careful observation, you'll soon work out a successful schedule.

Accidents, by the way, are just that—accidents. Clean them up

your puppy outside to relieve himself, use a one-word command such as "Outside" or "Go-potty" (that's one word to the puppy!) as you pick him up and attach his leash. Then put him down in his area. If he is too big for you to carry, snap the leash on quickly and lead him to his spot. Now comes the hard part—hard for you, that is. Just stand there until he

Whether during house-training or basic obedience lessons, a reward for correct behavior helps reinforce what you want your puppy to do.

quickly and thoroughly, without comment, after the puppy has been taken outside to finish his business and then put back into his area or crate. If you witness an accident in progress, say "No!" in a stern voice and get the pup outdoors immediately. No punishment is needed. You and your puppy are just learning each other's language, and sometimes it's easy to miss a puppy's message. Chalk it up to experience and watch more closely from now on.

**KEEPING THE PACK ORDERLY**

Discipline is a form of training that brings order to life. For example, military discipline is what allows the soldiers in an army to work as one. Discipline is a form of teaching and, in dogs, is the basis of how the successful pack operates. Each member knows his place in the pack and all respect the leader, or alpha dog. It is essential for your puppy that you establish this type of relationship, with you as the alpha, or leader. It is a form of social coexistence that all canines recognize and accept. Discipline, therefore, is never to be confused with punishment. When you teach your puppy how you want him to behave, and he behaves properly and you praise him for it, you are disciplining him with a form of positive reinforcement.

For a dog, rewards come in the form of praise, a smile, a cheerful

**TIPS FOR TRAINING AND SAFETY**

1. Whether on- or off-leash, practice only in a fenced area.
2. Remove the training collar when the training session is over.
3. Don't try to break up a dogfight.
4. "Come," "Leave it" and "Wait" are safety commands.
5. The dog belongs in a crate or behind a barrier when riding in the car.
6. Don't ignore the dog's first sign of aggression. Aggression only gets worse, so take it seriously.
7. Keep the faces of children and dogs separated.
8. Pay attention to what the dog is chewing.
9. Keep the vet's number near your phone.
10. "Okay" is a useful release command.

tone of voice, a few friendly pats or a rub of the ears. Rewards are also small food treats. Obviously, that does not mean bits of regular dog food. Instead, treats are very small bits of special things like cheese or pieces of soft dog treats. The idea is to reward the dog with something very small that he can taste and swallow, providing instant positive reinforcement. If he has to take time to chew the treat, he will have forgotten what he did to earn it by the time he is finished!

Your puppy should never be physically punished. The displeasure shown on your face and in your voice is sufficient to signal to the pup that he has done something wrong. He wants to please everyone higher up on the social ladder, especially his leader, so a scowl and harsh voice will take care of the error. Growling out the word "Shame!" when the pup is caught in the act of doing something wrong is better than the repetitive "No." Some dogs hear "No" so often that they begin to think it's their name! By the way, do not use the dog's name when you're correcting him. His name is reserved to get his attention for something pleasant about to take place.

There are punishments that have nothing to do with you. For example, your dog may think that chasing cats is one reason for his existence. You can try to stop it as much as you like but without success, because it's such fun for the dog. But one good hissing, spitting, swipe of a cat's claws across the dog's nose will put an end to the game forever. Intervene only when your dog's eyeball is seriously at risk. Cat scratches can cause permanent damage to an innocent but annoying puppy.

## PUPPY KINDERGARTEN

### COLLAR AND LEASH
Before you begin your Scottish Deerhound puppy's education, he must be used to his collar and leash. Choose a collar for your puppy that is secure, but not heavy or bulky. He won't enjoy training if he's uncomfortable. A flat buckle collar is fine for every-day wear and for initial puppy

All training should take place with your Scottish Deerhound on lead. Only attempt off-lead training in a securely fenced area.

## "SCHOOL" MODE
When is your puppy ready for a lesson? Maybe not always when you are. Attempting training with treats just before his mealtime is asking for disaster. Notice what times of day he performs best and make that Fido's school time.

training. For older dogs, there are several types of training collars such as the martingale, which is a double loop that tightens slightly around the neck, or the head collar, which is similar to a horse's halter. Sighthounds typically do not respond well to harsh training methods, so avoid choke collars. Ask your breeder or an experienced sighthound trainer about an appropriate training collar for your Deerhound.

A lightweight 6-foot woven cotton or nylon training leash is preferred by most trainers because it is easy to fold up in your hand and comfortable to hold because there is a certain amount of give to it. There are lessons where the dog will start off 6 feet away from you

**SMILE WHEN YOU ORDER ME AROUND!**

While trainers recommend practicing with your dog every day, it's perfectly acceptable to take a "mental health day" off. It's better not to train the dog on days when you're in a sour mood. Your bad attitude or lack of interest will be sensed by your dog, and he will respond accordingly. Studies show that dogs are well tuned in to their humans' emotions. Be conscious of how you use your voice when talking to your dog. Raising your voice or shouting will only erode your dog's trust in you as his trainer and master.

at the end of the leash. The leash used to take the puppy outside to relieve himself is shorter because you don't want him to roam away from his area. The shorter leash will also be the one to use when you walk the puppy.

If you've been wise enough to enroll in a puppy kindergarten training class, suggestions will be made as to the best collar and leash for your young puppy. I say "wise" because your puppy will be in a class with puppies in his age range (up to five months old) of all breeds and sizes. It's the perfect way for him to learn the right way (and the wrong way) to interact with other dogs as well as their people. You cannot teach your puppy how to interpret another dog's sign language. For a first-time puppy owner, these socialization classes are invaluable. For experienced dog owners, they are a real boon to further training.

**ATTENTION**
You've been using the dog's name since the minute you collected him from the breeder, so you should be able to get his attention by saying his name—with a big smile and in an excited tone of voice. His response will be the puppy equivalent of "Here I am! What are we going to do?" Your immediate response (if you haven't guessed by now) is "Good dog." Rewarding him at the moment he pays attention to you

front of you. Show him a treat in the palm of your right hand. Bring your hand up under his nose and, almost in slow motion, move your hand up and back so his nose goes up in the air and his head tilts back as he follows the treat in your hand. At that point, he will have to either sit or fall over, so as his back legs buckle under, say "Sit, good dog," and then give him the treat and lots of praise. You may have to begin with your hand lightly running up his chest, actually lifting his chin up until he sits. Some (usually older) dogs require gentle pressure on their hindquarters with the left hand, in which case the dog should be

In teaching the sit exercise, you may have to begin by guiding your dog into the sit position until he gets the idea.

teaches him the proper way to respond when he hears his name.

## EXERCISES FOR A BASIC CANINE EDUCATION

### THE SIT EXERCISE

There are several ways to teach the puppy to sit. The first one is to catch him whenever he is about to sit and, as his backside nears the floor, say "Sit, good dog!" That's positive reinforcement and, if your timing is sharp, he will learn that what he's doing at that second is connected to your saying "Sit" and that you think he's clever for doing it!

Another method is to start with the puppy on his leash in

Once the sit command is learned, practice it at the beginning and end of every lesson. Success builds confidence in the Scottish Deerhound pupil.

on your left side. Puppies generally do not appreciate this physical dominance.

After a few times, you should be able to show the dog a treat in the open palm of your hand, raise your hand waist-high as you say "Sit" and have him sit. Once again, you have taught him two things at the same time. Both the verbal command and the motion of the hand are signals for the sit. Your puppy is watching you almost more than he is listening to you, so what you do is just as important as what you say.

Don't save any of these drills only for training sessions. Use them as much as possible at odd times during a normal day. The dog should always sit before being given his food dish. He should sit to let you go through a doorway first, when the doorbell rings or when you stop to speak to someone on the street.

*A dog may be reluctant to assume the down position on command. He may need gentle guidance on your part, so you can see that it would be easier to teach this command to a puppy.*

### THE DOWN EXERCISE

Before beginning to teach the down command, you must consider how the dog feels about this exercise. To him, "down" is a submissive position. Being flat on the floor with you standing over him is not his idea of fun. It's up to you to let him know that, while it may not be fun, the reward of your approval is worth his effort.

Start with the puppy on your left side in a sit position. Hold the leash right above his collar in your left hand. Have an extra-special treat, such as a small piece of cooked chicken or hot dog, in your right hand. Place it at the end of the pup's nose and steadily move your hand down and forward along the ground. Hold the leash to prevent a sudden lunge for the food. As the puppy goes into the down position, say "Down" very gently.

The difficulty with this exercise is twofold: it's both the submissive aspect and the fact that most people say the word "Down" as if they were drill sergeants in charge of recruits! So issue the command sweetly, give him the treat and have the pup maintain the down position for several seconds. If he tries to get up immediately, place your hands on his shoulders and press down gently, giving him a very quiet "Good dog." As you progress with this lesson, increase the "down time" until he will hold it until you say "Okay" (his cue for release). Practice this one in the house at various times throughout the day.

By increasing the length of time during which the dog must maintain the down position, you'll find many uses for it. For example, he can lie at your feet in the vet's office or anywhere that both of you have to wait, when you are on the phone, while the family is eating and so forth. If you progress to training for competitive obedience, he'll already be all set for the exercise called the "long down."

**THE STAY EXERCISE**
You can teach your Scottish Deerhound to stay in the sit, down and stand positions. To teach the sit/stay, have the dog sit on your left side. Hold the leash at waist level in your left hand and let the dog know that you have a treat in your closed right hand. Step forward on your right foot as you say "Stay." Immediately turn and stand directly in front of the dog, keeping your right hand up high so he'll keep his eye on the treat hand and maintain the sit position for a count of five. Return to your original position and offer the reward.

Increase the length of the sit/stay each time until the dog can hold it for at least 30 seconds without moving. After about a

The verbal command "Stay" is reinforced with a hand signal.

week of success, move out on your right foot and take two steps before turning to face the dog. Give the "Stay" hand signal (left palm back toward the dog's head) as you leave. He gets the treat when you return and he holds the sit/stay. Increase the distance that you walk away from him before turning until you reach the length of your training leash. But don't rush it! Go back to the beginning if he moves before he should. No matter what the lesson, never be upset by having to back up for a few days. The repetition and practice are what will make your dog reliable in these commands. It won't do any good to move on to something more difficult if the

You want your Deerhound to come running enthusiastically when he hears you call him.

command is not mastered at the easier levels. Above all, even if you do get frustrated, never let your puppy know! Always keep a positive, upbeat attitude during training, which will transmit to your dog for positive results.

The down/stay is taught in the same way once the dog is completely reliable and steady with the down command. Again, don't rush it. With the dog in the down position on your left side, step out on your right foot as you say "Stay." Return by walking around in back of the dog and into your original position. While you are training, it's okay to murmur something like "Hold on" to encourage him to stay put. When the dog will stay without moving when you are at a distance of 3 or 4 feet, begin to increase the length of time before you return. Be sure he holds the down on your return until you say "Okay." At that point, he gets his treat—just so he'll remember for next time that it's not over until it's over.

### THE COME EXERCISE

No command is more important to the safety of your Scottish Deerhound than "Come," a command that is particularly challenging to teach to a sighthound. It is what you should say every single time you see the puppy running toward you: "Brodie, come! Good dog." During playtime, run a few feet away from the puppy and turn and tell him to "Come" as he is already running to you. You can go so far as to teach your puppy two things at once if you squat down and hold out your arms. As the pup gets close to you and you're saying "Good dog," bring your right arm in about waist high. Now he's also learning the hand signal, an excellent device should you be on the phone when you need to get him to come to you! You'll also both be one step ahead when you enter obedience classes.

When the puppy responds to your well-timed "Come," try it with the puppy on the training leash. This time, catch him off-guard, while he's sniffing a leaf or watching a bird: "Brodie, come!" You may have to pause for a split second after his name to be sure you have his attention. If the puppy shows any sign of confusion, give the leash a mild jerk and take a couple of steps backward. Do not repeat the command. In this case, you should say "Good come" as he reaches you.

That's the number-one rule of training. Each command word is given just once. Anything more is nagging. You'll also notice that all commands are one word only. Even when they are actually two words, you say them as one.

Never call the dog to come to you—with or without his name—if you are angry or intend to correct him for some misbehavior. When correcting the pup, you go to him. Your dog must always connect "Come" with something pleasant and with your approval; then you can rely on his response.

Puppies, like children, have notoriously short attention spans, so don't overdo it with any of the training. Keep each lesson short. Break it up with a quick run around the yard or a ball toss, repeat the lesson and quit as soon as the pup gets it right. That way, you will always end with a "Good dog."

Life isn't perfect and neither are puppies. A time will come, often around ten months of age, when he'll become "selectively deaf" or choose to "forget" his name. He may respond by wagging his tail (and even seeming to smile at you) with a look that says "Make me!" Laugh, throw his favorite toy and skip the lesson you had planned. Pups will be pups!

### THE HEEL EXERCISE

The second most important command to teach, after the come, is the heel. When you are walking your growing puppy, you need to be in control. Besides, it looks terrible to be pulled and yanked down the street, and it's not much fun either. Your eight- to ten-week-old puppy will probably follow you everywhere, but that's his natural instinct, not your control over the situation. However, any time he does follow you, you can say "Heel" and be ahead of the game, as he will learn to associate this command with the action of following you before you even begin teaching him to heel.

There is a very precise, almost military, procedure for teaching

With a dog as strong as the Deerhound, teaching your hound to behave properly on lead is essential.

This four-month-old puppy is practicing the heel exercise at a swift pace.

your dog to heel. As with all other obedience training, begin with the dog on your left side. He will be in a very nice sit and you will have the training leash across your chest. Hold the loop and folded leash in your right hand. Pick up the slack leash above the dog in your left hand and hold it loosely at your side. Step out on your left foot as you say "Heel." If the puppy does not move, give a gentle tug or pat your left leg to get him started. If he surges ahead of you, stop and pull him back gently until he is at your side. Tell him to sit and begin again.

Walk a few steps and stop while the puppy is correctly beside you. Tell him to sit and give mild verbal praise. (More enthusiastic praise will encourage him to think the lesson is over.) Repeat the lesson, increasing the number of steps you take only as long as the dog is heeling nicely beside you. When you end the

lesson, have him hold the sit, then give him the "Okay" to let him know that this is the end of the lesson. Praise him so that he knows he did a good job.

The cure for excessive pulling (a common problem) is to stop when the dog is no more than 2 or 3 feet ahead of you. Guide him back into position and begin again. With a really determined puller, try switching to a head collar. This will automatically turn the pup's head toward you so you can bring him back easily to the heel position. Give quiet, reassuring praise every time the leash goes slack and he's staying with you.

Staying and heeling can take a lot out of a dog, so provide playtime and free-running exercise to shake off the stress when the lessons are over. You don't want him to associate training with all work and no fun.

**TAPERING OFF TIDBITS**
Your dog has been watching you—and the hand that treats—throughout all of his lessons, and now it's time to break the treat habit. Begin by giving him treats at the end of each lesson only. Then start to give a treat after the end of only some of the lessons. At the end of every lesson, as well as during the lessons, be consistent with the praise. Your pup now doesn't know whether he'll get a treat or not, but he should keep performing well just in case!

Finally, you will stop giving treat rewards entirely. Save them for something brand-new that you want to teach him. Keep up the praise and you'll always have a "good dog."

## NO MORE TREATS!
When your dog is responding promptly and correctly to commands, it's time to eliminate treats. Begin by alternating a treat reward with a verbal-praise-only reward. Gradually eliminate all treats while increasing the frequency of praise. Overlook pleading eyes and expectant expressions, but if he's still watching your treat hand, you're on your way to using hand signals.

## OBEDIENCE CLASSES
The advantages of an obedience class are that your dog will have to learn amid the distractions of other people and dogs and that your mistakes will be quickly corrected by the trainer. Teaching your dog along with a qualified instructor and other handlers who may have more dog experience than you is another plus of the class environment. The instructor and other handlers can help you to find the most efficient way of teaching your dog a command or exercise. It's often easier to learn by other people's mistakes than your own. You will also learn all of the requirements for competitive obedience trials, in which you can earn titles and go on to advanced jumping and retrieving exercises, which are fun for many dogs. Obedience classes build the foundation needed for many other canine activities (in which we humans are allowed to participate, too!).

If you hope to show your Scottish Deerhound, handling classes and practice at home will help to prepare both of you for the ring.

A Scottish Deerhound in full flight in a coursing event is spectacular to watch.

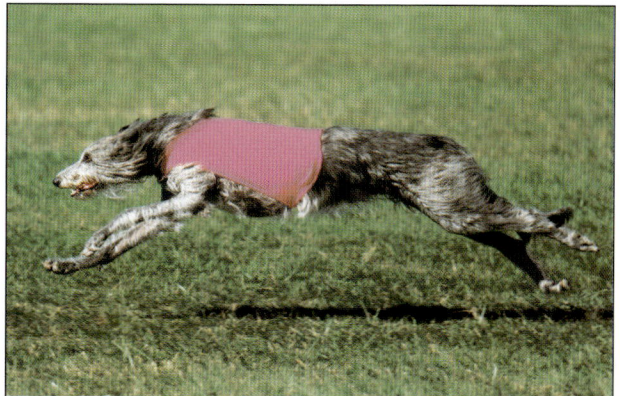

Tail

Croup

Hip

Loin

Back

Withers

Neck

Forehead

Muzzle

Shoulder

Forechest

Elbow

Brisket

Belly

Flank

Upper Thigh

Lower Thigh

Hock

Back Pastern

Hindfoot

Wrist

Front Pastern

Forefoot

# PHYSICAL STRUCTURE OF THE SCOTTISH DEERHOUND

# HEALTHCARE OF YOUR

# SCOTTISH DEERHOUND

By Lowell Ackerman, DVM, DACVD

## HEALTHCARE FOR A LIFETIME

When you own a dog, you become his healthcare advocate over his entire lifespan, as well as being the one to shoulder the financial burden of such care. Accordingly, it is worthwhile to focus on prevention rather than treatment, as you and your pet will both be happier.

Of course, the best place to have begun your program of preventive healthcare is with the initial purchase or adoption of your dog. There is no way of guaranteeing that your new furry friend is free of medical problems, but there are some things you can do to improve your odds. You certainly should have done adequate research into the Scottish Deerhound and have selected your puppy carefully rather than buying on impulse. Health issues aside, a large number of pet abandonment and relinquishment cases arise from a mismatch between pet needs and owner expectations. This is entirely preventable with appropriate planning and finding a good breeder.

Regarding healthcare issues specifically, it is very difficult to make blanket statements about where to acquire a problem-free pet, but, again, a reputable breeder is your best bet. In an ideal situation you have the opportunity to see both parents, get references from other owners of the breeder's pups and see genetic-testing documentation for several generations of the litter's ancestors. At the very least, you must thoroughly investigate your breed of interest and the problems inherent in that breed, as well as the genetic testing available to screen for those problems. Genetic testing offers some important benefits, but testing is available for only a few disorders in a relatively small number of breeds and is not available for some of the most common genetic diseases, such as hip dysplasia, cataracts, epilepsy, cardiomyopathy, etc. This area of research is indeed exciting and increasingly important, and advances will continue to be made each year. In fact, recent research has shown that there is an equivalent dog gene for 75% of known human genes, so research done in either species is likely to benefit the other.

We've also discussed that evaluating the behavioral nature of your Scottish Deerhound and that of his immediate family members is an important part of the selection process that cannot be underestimated or overemphasized. It is sometimes difficult to evaluate temperament in puppies because certain behavioral tendencies, such as some forms of aggression, may not be immediately evident. More dogs are euthanized each year for behavioral reasons than for all medical conditions combined, so it is critical to take temperament

### TAKING YOUR DOG'S TEMPERATURE

It is important to know how to take your dog's temperature at times when you think he may be ill. It's not the most enjoyable task, but it can be done without too much difficulty. It's easier with a helper, preferably someone with whom the dog is friendly, so that one of you can hold the dog while the other inserts the thermometer.

Before inserting the thermometer, coat the end with petroleum jelly. Insert the thermometer slowly and gently into the dog's rectum about one inch. Wait for the reading, about two minutes. Be sure to remove the thermometer carefully and clean it thoroughly after each use.

A dog's normal body temperature is between 100.5 and 102.5 degrees F. Immediate veterinary attention is required if the dog's temperature is below 99 or above 104 degrees F.

issues seriously. Start with a well-balanced, friendly companion and put the time and effort into proper socialization, and you will both be rewarded with a lifelong valued relationship.

Assuming that you have started off with a pup from healthy, sound stock, you then become responsible for helping your veterinarian keep your pet healthy. Some crucial things happen before you even bring your puppy home. Parasite control typically begins at two weeks of age, and vaccinations typically begin at six to eight weeks of age. A pre-pubertal evaluation is typically scheduled for about six months of age. At this time, a dental evaluation is done (since the adult teeth are now in), heartworm prevention is started and neutering or spaying is most commonly done.

It is critical to commence regular dental care at home if you have not already done so. It may not sound very important, but most dogs have active periodontal disease by four years of age if they don't have their teeth cleaned regularly at home, not just at their veterinary exams. Dental problems lead to more than just bad "doggy breath." Gum disease can have very serious medical consequences. If you start brushing your dog's teeth and using antiseptic rinses from a young age, your dog will be accustomed to it and will not resist. The results will be healthy dentition, which your pet will need to enjoy a long, healthy life.

Most dogs are considered adults at a year of age, although most larger breeds continue filling out until about two or so years old. Even individual dogs within each breed have different healthcare requirements, so work with your veterinarian to determine what will be needed and what your role should be. This doctor-client relationship is important because as vaccination guidelines change, there may not be an annual "vaccine visit" scheduled. You must make sure that you see your veterinarian at least annually, even if no vaccines are due, because this is the best opportunity to coordinate healthcare activities and to make sure that no medical issues creep by unaddressed.

At the senior stage in your Scottish Deerhound's life, your veterinarian will want to schedule visits twice yearly, instead of once, to run some laboratory screenings, electrocardiograms and the like, and perhaps to change the diet to something more digestible. Catching problems early is the best way to manage them effectively. Treating the early stages of heart disease is so much easier than trying to intervene when there is more significant damage to the heart muscle. Similarly,

managing the beginning of kidney problems is fairly routine if there is no significant kidney damage. Other problems, like cognitive dysfunction (similar to senility and Alzheimer's disease), cancer, diabetes and arthritis, are more common in older dogs, but all can be treated to help the dog live as many happy, comfortable years as possible. Just as in people, medical management is more effective (and less expensive) when you catch things early.

**SELECTING A VETERINARIAN**
There is probably no more important decision that you will make regarding your pet's healthcare than the selection of his doctor. Your pet's veterinarian will be a pediatrician, family-practice physician and gerontologist, depending on the dog's life stage, and will be the individual who makes recommendations regarding issues such as when specialists need to be consulted, when diagnostic testing and/or therapeutic intervention is needed and when you will need to seek outside emergency and critical-care services. Your vet will act as your advocate and liaison throughout these processes.

Everyone has his own idea about what to look for in a vet, an individual who will play a big role in his dog's (and, of course, his own) life for many years to come. For some, it is the compassionate caregiver with whom they hope to develop a professional relationship to span the lifetime of their dogs and even their future pets. For others, they are seeking a clinician with keen diagnostic and therapeutic insight who can deliver state-of-the-art healthcare. Still others need a veterinary facility that is open evenings and weekends, is in close proximity or provides mobile veterinary services to accommodate their schedules; these people may not much mind that their dogs might see different veterinarians on each visit. Just as we have different reasons for selecting our own healthcare professionals (e.g., covered by insurance plan, expert in field, convenient location, etc.), we should not expect that there is a one-size-fits-all recommendation for selecting a veterinarian and veterinary practice. The best advice is to be honest in your assessment of what you expect from a veterinary practice and to conscientiously research the options in your area. You will quickly appreciate that not all veterinary practices are the same, and you will be happiest with one that truly meets your needs.

There is another point to be considered in the selection of veterinary services. Not that long ago, a single veterinarian would attempt to manage all medical and surgical issues as they arose. That was often problematic because veterinarians are trained in many species and many diseases, and it was just impossible for general veterinary practitioners to be experts in every species, every breed, every field and every ailment. However, just as in the human healthcare fields, specialization has allowed general practitioners to concentrate on primary

## PROBLEM: AND THAT STARTS WITH "P"

Urinary tract problems more commonly affect female dogs, especially those who have been spayed. The first sign that a urinary tract problem exists usually is a strong odor from the urine or an unusual color. Blood in the urine, known as hematuria, is another sign of an infection, related to cystitis, a bladder infection, bladder cancer or a blood-clotting disorder. Urinary tract problems can also be signaled by the dog's straining while urinating, experiencing pain during urination and genital discharge as well as excessive water intake and urination.

Excessive drinking, in and of itself, does not indicate a urinary tract problem. A dog who is drinking more than normal may have a kidney or liver problem, a hormonal disorder or diabetes mellitus. Behaviorists report a disorder known as psychogenic polydipsia, which manifests itself in excessive drinking and urination. If you notice your dog drinking much more than normal, take him to the vet.

healthcare delivery, especially wellness and the prevention of infectious diseases, and to utilize a network of specialists to assist in the management of conditions that require specific expertise and experience. Thus there are now many types of veterinary specialists, including dermatologists, cardiologists, ophthalmologists, surgeons, internists, oncologists, neurologists, behaviorists, criticalists and others to help primary-care veterinarians deal with complicated medical challenges. In most cases, specialists see cases referred by primary-care veterinarians, make diagnoses and set up management plans. From there, the animals' ongoing care is returned to their primary-care veterinarians. This important team approach to your pet's medical-care needs has provided opportunities for advanced care and an unparalleled level of quality to be delivered.

With all of the opportunities for your Scottish Deerhound to receive high-quality veterinary medical care, there is another topic that needs to be addressed at the same time—cost. It's been said that you can have excellent healthcare or inexpensive healthcare, but never both; this is as true in veterinary medicine as it is in human medicine. While veterinary costs are a fraction of what the same services cost in the human health-care arena, it is still difficult to deal with unanticipated medical

**YOUR DOG NEEDS TO VISIT THE VET IF:**
- He has ingested a toxin such as antifreeze or a toxic plant; in these cases, administer first aid and call the vet right away
- His teeth are discolored, loose or missing or he has sores or other signs of infection or abnormality in the mouth
- He has been vomiting, has had diarrhea or has been constipated for over 24 hours; call immediately if you notice blood
- He has refused food for over 24 hours
- His eating habits, water intake or toilet habits have noticeably changed; if you have noticed weight gain or weight loss
- He shows symptoms of bloat, which requires *immediate* attention
- He is salivating excessively
- He has a lump in his throat
- He has a lump or bumps anywhere on the body
- He is very lethargic
- He appears to be in pain or otherwise has trouble chewing or swallowing
- His skin loses elasticity

Of course, there will be other instances in which a visit to the vet is necessary; these are just some of the signs that could be indicative of serious problems that need to be caught as early as possible.

costs, especially since they can easily creep into hundreds or even thousands of dollars if specialists or emergency services become involved. However, there are ways of managing these risks. The easiest is to buy pet health insurance and realize that its foremost purpose is not to cover routine healthcare visits but rather to serve as an umbrella for those rainy days when your pet needs medical care and you don't want to worry about whether or not you can afford that care.

Pet insurance policies are very cost-effective (and very inexpensive by human health-insurance standards), but make sure that you buy the policy long before you intend to use it (preferably starting in puppyhood because coverage will exclude pre-existing conditions) and that you are actually buying an indemnity insurance plan from an insurance company that is regulated by your state or province. Many insurance policy look-alikes are actually discount clubs that are redeemable only at specific locations and for specific services. An indemnity plan covers your pet at almost all veterinary, specialty and emergency practices and is an excellent way to manage your pet's ongoing healthcare needs.

## VACCINATIONS AND INFECTIOUS DISEASES

There has never been an easier time to prevent a variety of infectious diseases in your dog, but the advances we've made in veterinary medicine come with a price—choice. Now while it may seem that this choice is a good thing (and it is), it also has never been more difficult for the pet owner (or the veterinarian) to make an informed decision about the best way to protect pets through vaccination.

Years ago, it was just accepted that puppies got a starter series of vaccinations and then annual "boosters" throughout their lives to keep them protected. As more and more vaccines became available, consumers wanted the convenience of having all of that protection in a single injection. The result was "multivalent" vaccines that crammed a lot of protection into a single syringe. The manufacturers' recommendations were to give the vaccines annually, and this was a simple enough protocol to follow. However, as veterinary medicine has become more sophisticated and we have started looking more at healthcare quandaries rather than convenience, it became necessary to reevaluate the situation and deal with some tough questions. It is important to realize that whether or not to use a particular vaccine depends on the risk of contracting the disease against which it protects, the severity of the disease if it is contracted, the duration of immunity provided by the vaccine, the safety of the product and the needs of the individual animal. In a very general sense, rabies, distemper, hepatitis and parvovirus are considered core vaccine needs, while para-influenza, *Bordetella bronchiseptica*, leptospirosis, coronavirus and borreliosis (Lyme disease) are considered non-core needs and best reserved for animals that demonstrate reasonable risk of contracting the diseases.

### NEUTERING/SPAYING

Sterilization procedures (neutering for males/spaying for females) are meant to accomplish several purposes. While the underlying premise is to address the risk of pet overpopulation, there are also some medical and behavioral benefits to the surgeries as well. For females, spaying prior to the first estrus (heat cycle) leads to a marked reduction in the risk of mammary cancer and eliminates the risk of uterine problems. There also will be no manifestations of "heat" to attract male dogs and no bleeding in the house. For males, there is prevention of testicular cancer and a reduction in the risk of prostate problems. In both sexes there may be some limited reduc-

## THE SCOTTISH DEERHOUND CLUB OF AMERICA'S HEALTH SURVEY

To its great credit, the SDCA has worked hard to create reliable data about the health problems that concern the breed. It is generally accepted that gastric torsion (bloat), osteosarcoma (bone cancer) and cardiomyopathy (heart disease) have been important health problems, and in the 1990s the SDCA's Health and Genetics Committee collected data on more than 450 Deerhounds. The results of this survey yielded a database of information to include sex, date of birth and death, mature height and weight, cause of death, health problems experienced, and the age of onset for each health problem. In addition, the survey contains highly important information on adverse reaction to vaccines, vaccine failures, anesthesia-related adverse experiences, anesthetic regimens that worked well and drug-related adverse reactions. All this data will be of enormous benefit to the breed, and the club deserves hearty congratulations on its achievement.

It has been determined that 27% of Scottish Deerhound deaths are the result of heart or circulatory problems, while tumors or cancers account for 16%. In these cases the average age of death is around nine years of age. Further, the survey showed that 12% of Deerhounds die simply from age-related debility, in these cases the average age of death is 12 years. Gastric torsion accounts for 10% of deaths; the average age of death is about four and a half years.

It is reassuring to know that a number of Deerhounds die simply from "old age." Undoubtedly Deerhound breeders and owners around the world are grateful to the SDCA for having carried out such intricate research.

# COMMON INFECTIOUS DISEASES

Let's discuss some of the diseases that create the need for vaccination in the first place. Following are the major canine infectious diseases and a simple explanation of each.

**Rabies:** A devastating viral disease that can be fatal in dogs and people. In fact, vaccination of dogs and cats is an important public-health measure to create a resistant animal buffer population to protect people from contracting the disease. Vaccination schedules are determined on a government level and are not optional for pet owners; rabies vaccination is required by law in all 50 states.

**Parvovirus:** A severe, potentially life-threatening disease that is easily transmitted between dogs. There are four strains of the virus, but it is believed that there is significant "cross-protection" between strains that may be included in individual vaccines.

**Distemper:** A potentially severe and life-threatening disease with a relatively high risk of exposure, especially in certain regions. In very high-risk distemper environments, young pups may be vaccinated with human measles vaccine, a related virus that offers cross-protection when administered at four to ten weeks of age.

**Hepatitis**: Caused by canine adenovirus type 1 (CAV-1), but since vaccination with the causative virus has a higher rate of adverse effects, cross-protection is derived from the use of adenovirus type 2 (CAV-2), a cause of respiratory disease and one of the potential causes of canine cough. Vaccination with CAV-2 provides long-term immunity against hepatitis, but relatively less protection against respiratory infection.

**Canine cough:** Also called tracheobronchitis, actually a fairly complicated result of viral and bacterial offenders; therefore, even with vaccination, protection is incomplete. Wherever dogs congregate, canine cough will likely be spread among them. Intranasal vaccination with *Bordetella* and parainfluenza is the best safeguard, but the duration of immunity does not appear to be very long, typically a year at most. These are non-core vaccines, but vaccination is sometimes mandated by boarding kennels, obedience classes, dog shows and other places where dogs congregate to try to minimize spread of infection.

**Leptospirosis:** A potentially fatal disease that is more common in some geographic regions. It is capable of being spread to humans. The disease varies with the individual "serovar," or strain, of *Leptospira* involved. Since there does not appear to be much cross-protection between serovars, protection is only as good as the likelihood that the serovar in the vaccine is the same as the one in the pet's local environment. Problems with *Leptospira* vaccines are that protection does not last very long, side effects are not uncommon and a large percentage of dogs (perhaps 30%) may not respond to vaccination.

***Borrelia burgdorferi:*** The cause of Lyme disease, the risk of which varies with the geographic area in which the pet lives and travels. Lyme disease is spread by deer ticks in the eastern US and western black-legged ticks in the western part of the country, and the risk of exposure is high in some regions. Lameness, fever and inappetence are most commonly seen in affected dogs. The extent of protection from the vaccine has not been conclusively demonstrated.

**Coronavirus:** This disease has a high risk of exposure, especially in areas where dogs congregate, but it typically causes only mild to moderate digestive upset (diarrhea, vomiting, etc.). Vaccines are available, but the duration of protection is believed to be relatively short and the effectiveness of the vaccine in preventing infection is considered low.

There are many other vaccinations available, including those for *Giardia* and canine adenovirus-1. While there may be some specific indications for their use, and local risk factors to be considered, they are not widely recommended for most dogs.

tion in aggressive behaviors toward other dogs, and some diminishing of urine marking, roaming and mounting.

While neutering and spaying do indeed prevent animals from contributing to pet overpopulation, even no-cost and low-cost neutering options have not eliminated the problem. Perhaps one of the main reasons for this is that individuals that intentionally breed their dogs and those that allow their animals to run at large are the main causes of unwanted offspring. Also, animals in shelters are often there because they were abandoned or relinquished, not because they came from unplanned matings. Neutering/ spaying is important, but it should be considered in the context of the real causes of animals' ending up in shelters and eventually being euthanized.

One of the important considerations regarding neutering is that it is a surgical procedure. This sometimes gets lost in discussions of low-cost procedures and commoditization of the process. In females, spaying is specifically referred to as an ovariohysterectomy. In this procedure, a midline incision is made in the abdomen and the entire uterus and both ovaries are surgically removed. While this is a major invasive surgical procedure, it usually has few complications because it is typically performed on healthy young animals. However, it is major surgery, as any woman who has had a hysterectomy will attest.

In males, neutering has traditionally referred to castration, which involves the surgical removal of both testicles. While still a significant piece of surgery, there is not the abdominal exposure that is required in the female surgery. In addition, there is now a chemical sterilization option in which a solution is injected into each testicle, leading to atrophy of the sperm-producing cells. This can typically be done under sedation rather than full anesthesia. This is a relatively new approach, and there are no long-term clinical studies yet available.

Neutering/spaying is typically done around six months of age at most veterinary hospitals, although techniques have been pioneered to perform the procedures in animals as young as eight weeks of age. In general, the surgeries on the very young animals are done for the specific reason of sterilizing them before they go to their new homes. This is done in some shelter hospitals for assurance that the animals will definitely not produce any pups. Otherwise, these organizations need to rely on owners to comply with their wishes to have the animals "altered" at a later date, something that does not always happen.

# THE ABCs OF
# Emergency Care

## Abrasions
Clean wound with running water or 3% hydrogen peroxide. Pat dry with gauze and spray with antibiotic. Do not cover.

## Animal Bites
Clean area with soap and saline solution or water. Apply pressure to any bleeding area. Apply antibiotic ointment. Identify biting animal and contact vet.

## Antifreeze Poisoning
Induce vomiting and take dog to the vet.

## Bee Sting
Remove stinger and apply soothing lotion or cold compress; give antihistamine in proper dosage.

## Bleeding
Apply pressure directly to wound with gauze or towel for five to ten minutes. If wound does not stop bleeding, wrap wound with gauze and adhesive tape.

## Bloat/Gastric Torsion
*Immediately* take the dog to the vet or emergency clinic; phone from car. No time to waste.

## Burns
**Chemical:** Bathe dog with water and pet shampoo. Rinse in saline solution. Apply antibiotic ointment.

**Acid:** Rinse with water. Apply one part baking soda, two parts water to affected area.

**Alkali:** Rinse with water. Apply one part vinegar, four parts water to affected area.

**Electrical:** Apply antibiotic ointment. Seek veterinary assistance immediately.

## Choking
If the dog is on the verge of collapsing, wedge a solid object, such as the handle of a screwdriver, between molars on one side of mouth to keep mouth open. Pull tongue out. Use long-nosed pliers or fingers to remove foreign object. Do not push the object down the dog's throat. For small or medium dogs, hold dog upside down by hind legs and shake firmly to dislodge foreign object.

## Chlorine Ingestion
With clean water, rinse the mouth and eyes. Give dog water to drink; contact the vet.

## Constipation
Feed dog 2 tablespoons bran flakes with each meal. Encourage drinking water. Mix $1/4$-teaspoon mineral oil in dog's food.

## Diarrhea
Withhold food for 12 to 24 hours. Feed dog anti-diarrheal with eyedropper. When feeding resumes, feed one part boiled hamburger, one part plain cooked rice, $1/4$ to $3/4$ cup four times daily.

## Dog Bite
Snip away hair around puncture wound; clean with 3% hydrogen peroxide; apply tincture of iodine. Identify biting dog and call the vet. If wound appears deep, take the dog to the vet.

## Frostbite
Wrap the dog in a heavy blanket. Warm affected area with a warm bath for ten minutes. Red color to skin will return with circulation; if tissues are pale after 20 minutes, contact the vet.

## Heat Stroke

Submerge the dog (up to his muzzle) in cold water; if no response within ten minutes, contact the vet.

## Hot Spots

Mix 2 packets Domeboro® with 2 cups water. Saturate cloth with mixture and apply to hot spots for 15–30 minutes. Apply antibiotic ointment. Repeat every six to eight hours.

## Poisonous Plants

Wash affected area with soap and water. Cleanse with alcohol. For foxtail/grass, apply antibiotic ointment. Contact vet if plant is ingested.

## Rat Poison Ingestion

Induce vomiting. Keep dog calm, maintain dog's normal body temperature (use blanket or heating pad). Get to the vet for antidote.

## Shock

Keep the dog calm and warm; call for veterinary assistance.

## Snake Bite

If possible, bandage the area and apply pressure. If the area is not conducive to bandaging, use ice to control bleeding. Get immediate help from the vet.

## Tick Removal

Apply flea and tick spray directly on tick. Wait one minute. Using tweezers or wearing plastic gloves, grasp the tick's body firmly. Apply antibiotic ointment.

## Vomiting

Restrict water intake; offer a few ice cubes. Withhold food for next meal. Contact vet if vomiting (or diarrhea/constipation) persists longer than 24 hours.

*Use a portable, durable container large enough to contain all items.*

# DOG OWNER'S FIRST-AID KIT

❑ **Gauze bandages/swabs**
❑ **Adhesive and non-adhesive bandages**
❑ **Antibiotic powder**
❑ **Antiseptic wash**
❑ **Hydrogen peroxide 3%**
❑ **Antibiotic ointment**
❑ **Lubricating jelly**
❑ **Rectal thermometer**
❑ **Nylon muzzle**
❑ **Scissors and forceps**
❑ **Eyedropper**
❑ **Syringe**
❑ **Anti-bacterial/fungal solution**
❑ **Saline solution**
❑ **Antihistamine**
❑ **Cotton balls**
❑ **Nail clippers**
❑ **Screwdriver/pen knife**
❑ **Flashlight**
❑ **Emergency phone numbers**

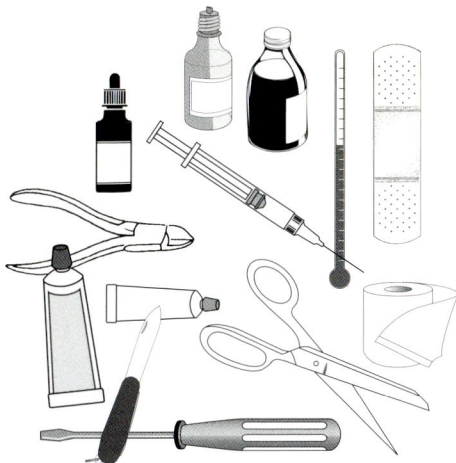

## EXTERNAL PARASITES

### FLEAS

Fleas have been around for millions of years and, while we have better tools now for controlling them than at any time in the past, there still is little chance that they will end up on an endangered species list. Actually, they are very well adapted to living on our pets, and they continue to adapt as we make advances.

The female flea can consume 15 times her weight in blood during active reproduction and can lay as many as 40 eggs a day. These eggs are very resistant to the effects of insecticides. They hatch into larvae, which then mature and spin cocoons. The immature fleas reside in this pupal stage until the time is right for feeding. This pupal stage is also very resistant to the effects of insecticides, and pupae can last in the environment without feeding for many months. Newly emergent fleas are attracted to animals by the warmth of the animals' bodies, movement and exhaled carbon dioxide. However, when they first emerge from their cocoons, they orient towards light; thus when an animal passes between a flea and the light source, casting a shadow, the flea pounces and starts to feed. If the animal turns out to be a dog or cat, the reproductive cycle continues. If the flea lands on another type of animal, including a person, the flea will bite but will then look for a more appropriate host. An emerging adult flea can survive without feeding for up to 12 months but, once it tastes blood, it can survive off its host for only 3 to 4 days.

It was once thought that fleas spend most of their lives in the environment, but we now know that fleas won't willingly jump off a dog unless leaping to another dog or when physically removed by brushing, bathing or other manipulation. Flea eggs, on the other hand, are shiny and smooth, and they roll off the animal and into the environment. The eggs, larvae and pupae then exist in the environment, but once the adult finds a susceptible animal, it's home sweet home until the flea is forced to seek refuge elsewhere.

Since adult fleas live on the animal and immature forms survive in the environment, a successful treatment plan must address all stages of the flea life cycle. There are now several safe and effective flea-control products that can be applied on a monthly

**FLEA PREVENTION FOR YOUR DOG**

- Discuss with your veterinarian the safest product to protect your dog, likely in the form of a monthly tablet or a liquid preparation placed on the back of the dog's neck.
- For dogs suffering from flea-bite dermatitis, a shampoo or topical insecticide treatment is required.
- Your lawn and property should be sprayed with an insecticide designed to kill fleas and ticks that lurk outdoors.
- Using a flea comb, check the dog's coat regularly for any signs of parasites.
- Practice good housekeeping. Vacuum floors, carpets and furniture regularly, especially in the areas that the dog frequents, and wash the dog's bedding weekly.
- Follow up house-cleaning with carpet shampoos and sprays to rid the house of fleas at all stages of development. Insect growth regulators are the safest option.

basis. These include fipronil, imidacloprid, selamectin and permethrin (found in several formulations). Most of these products have significant flea-killing rates within 24 hours. However, none of them will control the immature forms in the environment. To accomplish this, there are a variety of insect growth regulators that can be sprayed into

## THE FLEA'S LIFE CYCLE

What came first, the flea or the egg? This age-old mystery is more difficult to comprehend than the actual cycle of the flea. Fleas usually live only about four months. A female can lay 2,000 eggs in her lifetime.

*PHOTO BY CAROLINA BIOLOGICAL SUPPLY CO.*

**Egg**

After ten days of rolling around your carpet or under your furniture, the eggs hatch into larvae, which feed on various and sundry debris. In days or months, depending on the climate, the larvae spin cocoons and develop into the pupal or nymph stage, which quickly develop into fleas.

**Larva**

*PHOTO BY CAROLINA BIOLOGICAL SUPPLY CO.*

**Pupa**

These immature fleas must locate a host within 10 to 14 days or they will die. Only about 1% of the flea population exist as adult fleas, while the other 99% exist as eggs, larvae or pupae.

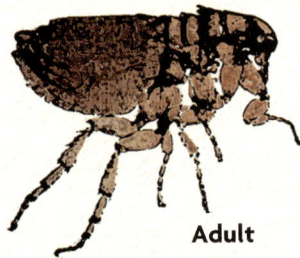

**Adult**

## KILL FLEAS THE NATURAL WAY

If you choose not to go the route of conventional medication, there are some natural ways to ward off fleas:

- Dust your dog with a natural flea powder, composed of such herbal goodies as rosemary, wormwood, pennyroyal, citronella, rue, tobacco powder and eucalyptus.
- Apply diatomaceous earth, the fossilized remains of single-cell algae, to your carpets, furniture and pet's bedding. Even though it's not good for dogs, it's even worse for fleas, which will dry up swiftly and die.
- Brush your dog frequently, give him adequate exercise and let him fast occasionally. All of these activities strengthen the dog's immune system and make him more resistant to disease and parasites.
- Bathe your dog with a capful of pennyroyal or eucalyptus oil.
- Feed a natural diet, free of additives and preservatives. Add some fresh garlic and brewer's yeast to the dog's morning portion, as these items have flea-repelling properties.

the environment (e.g., pyriprox-yfen, methoprene, fenoxycarb) as well as insect development inhibitors such as lufenuron that can be administered. These compounds have no effect on adult fleas, but they stop immature forms from developing into adults. In years gone by, we relied heavily on toxic insecticides (such as organophosphates, organochlorines and carbamates) to manage the flea problem, but today's options are not only much safer to use on our pets but also safer for the environment.

## TICKS

Ticks are members of the spider class (arachnids) and are blood-sucking parasites capable of trans-mitting a variety of diseases, including Lyme disease, ehrlichio-sis, babesiosis and Rocky Mountain spotted fever. It's easy to see ticks on your own skin, but it is more of a challenge when your furry companion is affected. Whenever you happen to be plan-ning a stroll in a tick-infested area (especially forests, grassy or wooded areas or parks) be prepared to do a thorough inspec-tion of your dog afterward to search for ticks. Ticks can be tricky, so make sure you spend time looking in the ears, between the toes and everywhere else where a tick might hide. Ticks need to be attached for 24–72 hours before they transmit most of the diseases that they carry, so you do have a window of oppor-tunity for some preventive intervention.

### A TICKING BOMB

There is nothing good about a tick's harpooning his nose into your dog's skin. Among the diseases caused by ticks are Rocky Mountain spotted fever, canine ehrlichiosis, canine babesiosis, canine hepatozoonosis and Lyme disease. If a dog is allergic to the saliva of a female wood tick, he can develop tick paralysis.

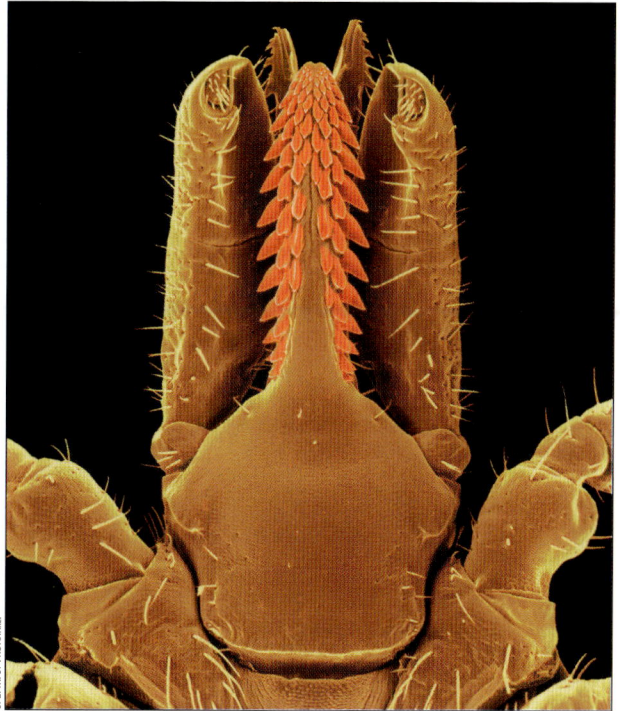

S. E. M. BY PHOTOTAKE.

Female ticks live to eat and breed. They can lay between 4,000 and 5,000 eggs and they die soon after. Males, on the other hand, live only to mate with the females and continue the process as long as they are able. Most ticks live on multiple hosts before parasitizing dogs. The immature forms typically reside on grass and shrubs, waiting for suscepti-ble animals to walk by. The larvae and nymph stages typically feed on wildlife.

If only a few ticks are present on a dog, they can be plucked out, but it is important to remove the entire head and mouthparts,

A scanning electron micrograph of the head of a female deer tick, *Ixodes dammini*, a parasitic tick that carries Lyme disease.

Deer tick,
*Ixodes dammini.*

PHOTO BY CAROLINA BIOLOGICAL SUPPLY CO.

of in a container of alcohol or household bleach.

Some of the newer flea products, specifically those with fipronil, selamectin and permethrin, have effect against some, but not all, species of tick. Flea collars containing appropriate pesticides (e.g., propoxur, chlorfenvinphos) can aid in tick control. In most areas, such collars should be placed on animals in March, at the beginning of the tick season, and changed regularly. Leaving the collar on when the pesticide level is waning invites the development of resistance. Amitraz collars are also good for tick control, and the active ingredient does not interfere with other flea-control products. The ingredient helps prevent the attachment of ticks to the skin and will cause those ticks already on the skin to detach themselves.

which may be deeply embedded in the skin. This is best accomplished with forceps designed especially for this purpose; fingers can be used but should be protected with rubber gloves, plastic wrap or at least a paper towel. The tick should be grasped as closely as possible to the animal's skin and should be pulled upward with steady, even pressure. Do not squeeze, crush or puncture the body of the tick or you risk exposure to any disease carried by that tick. Once the ticks have been removed, the sites of attachment should be disinfected. Your hands should then be washed with soap and water to further minimize risk of contagion. The tick should be disposed

### TICK CONTROL

Removal of underbrush and leaf litter and the thinning of trees in areas where tick control is desired are recommended. These actions remove the cover and food sources for small animals that serve as hosts for ticks. With continued mowing of grasses in these areas, the probability of ticks' surviving is further reduced. A variety of insecticide ingredients (e.g., resmethrin, carbaryl, permethrin, chlorpyrifos, dioxathion and allethrin) are registered for tick control around the home.

## MITES

Mites are tiny arachnid parasites that parasitize the skin of dogs. Skin diseases caused by mites are referred to as "mange," and there are many different forms seen in dogs. These forms are very different from one another, each one warranting an individual description.

Sarcoptic mange, or scabies, is one of the itchiest conditions that affects dogs. The microscopic *Sarcoptes* mites burrow into the superficial layers of the skin and can drive dogs crazy with itchiness. They are also communicable to people, although they can't complete their reproductive cycle on people. In addition to being tiny, the mites also are often difficult to find when trying to make a diagnosis. Skin scrapings from multiple areas are examined microscopically but, even then, sometimes the mites cannot be found.

Fortunately, scabies is relatively easy to treat, and there are a variety of products that will successfully kill the mites. Since the mites can't live in the environment for very long without feeding, a complete cure is usually possible within four to eight weeks.

Cheyletiellosis is caused by a relatively large mite, which sometimes can be seen even without a microscope. Often referred to as "walking dandruff," this also causes itching, but not usually as profound as with scabies. While *Cheyletiella* mites can survive somewhat longer

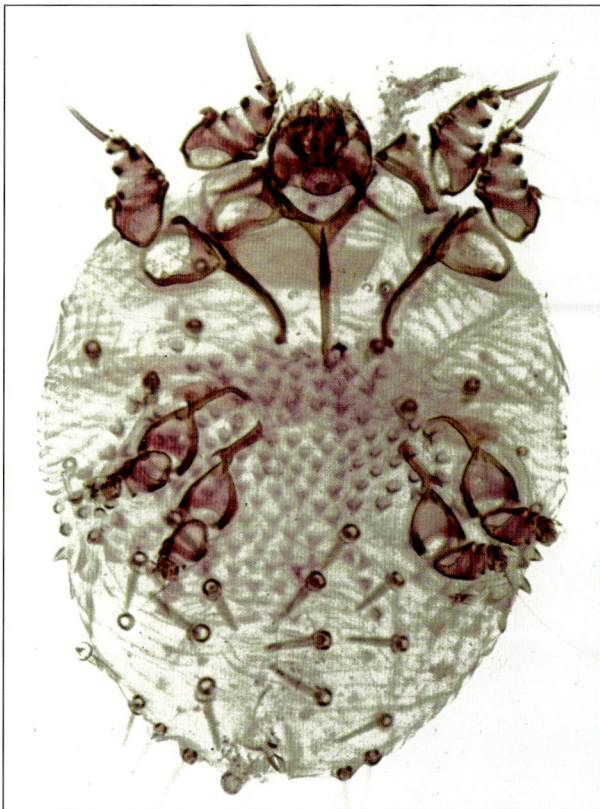

PHOTO BY PHOTOTAKE.

in the environment than scabies mites, they too are relatively easy to treat, being responsive to not only the medications used to treat scabies but also often to flea-control products.

*Otodectes cynotis* is the canine ear mite and is one of the more common causes of mange, especially in young dogs in shelters or pet stores. That's because the mites are typically present in large numbers and are quickly spread to nearby animals. The mites rarely do much harm but can be difficult

**Sarcoptes scabiei,** commonly known as the "itch mite."

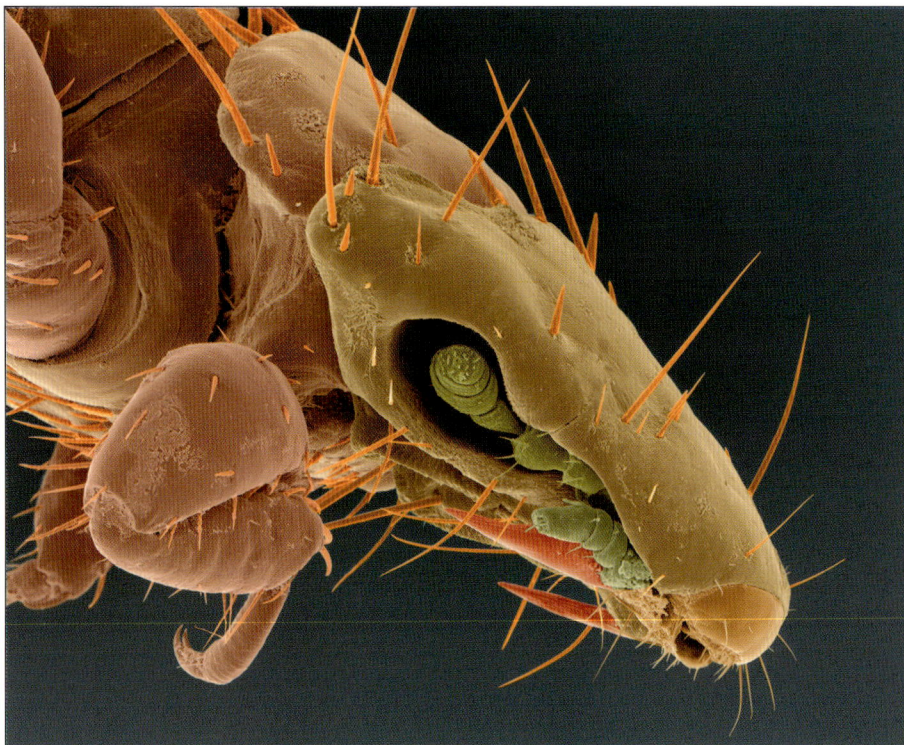

Micrograph of a dog louse, *Heterodoxus spiniger*. Female lice attach their eggs to the hairs of the dog. As the eggs hatch, the larval lice bite and feed on the blood. Lice can also feed on dead skin and hair. This feeding activity can cause hair loss and skin problems.

S. E. M. BY DR. DENNIS KUNKEL, UNIVERSITY OF HAWAII.

to eradicate if the treatment regimen is not comprehensive. While many try to treat the condition with ear drops only, this is the most common cause of treatment failure. Ear drops cause the mites to simply move out of the ears and as far away as possible (usually to the base of the tail) until the insecticide levels in the ears drop to an acceptable level—then it's back to business as usual! The successful treatment of ear mites requires treating all animals in the household with a systemic insecticide, such as selamectin, or a combination of miticidal ear drops combined with whole-body flea-control preparations.

Demodicosis, sometimes referred to as red mange, can be one of the most difficult forms of mange to treat. Part of the problem has to do with the fact that the mites live in the hair follicles and they are relatively well shielded from topical and systemic products. The main issue, however, is that demodectic mange typically results only when there is some underlying process interfering with the dog's immune system.

Since *Demodex* mites are normal residents of the skin of

mammals, including humans, there is usually a mite population explosion only when the immune system fails to keep the number of mites in check. In young animals, the immune deficit may be transient or may reflect an actual inherited immune problem. In older animals, demodicosis is usually seen only when there is another disease hampering the immune system, such as diabetes, cancer, thyroid problems or the use of immune-suppressing drugs. Accordingly, treatment involves not only trying to kill the mange mites but also discerning what is interfering with immune function and correcting it if possible.

Chiggers represent several different species of mite that don't parasitize dogs specifically, but do latch on to passersby and can cause irritation. The problem is most prevalent in wooded areas in the late summer and fall. Treatment is not difficult, as the mites do not complete their life cycle on dogs and are susceptible to a variety of miticidal products.

### MOSQUITOES

Mosquitoes have long been known to transmit a variety of diseases to people, as well as just being biting pests during warm weather. They also pose a real risk to pets. Not only do they carry deadly heartworms but

recently there also has been much concern over their involvement with West Nile virus. While we can avoid heartworm with the use of preventive medications, there are no such preventives for West Nile virus. The only method of prevention in endemic areas is active mosquito control. Fortunately, most dogs that have been exposed to the virus only developed flu-like symptoms and, to date, there have not been the large number of reported deaths in canines as seen in some other species.

Illustration of *Demodex folliculoram.*

### MOSQUITO REPELLENT

Low concentrations of DEET (less than 10%), found in many human mosquito repellents, have been safely used on dogs but, in these concentrations, probably give only about two hours of protection. DEET may be safe in these small concentrations, but since it is not licensed for use on dogs, there is no research proving its safety for dogs. Products containing permethrin give the longest-lasting protection, perhaps two to four weeks. As DEET is not licensed for use on dogs, and both DEET and permethrin can be quite toxic to cats, appropriate care should be exercised. Other products, such as those containing oil of citronella, also have some mosquito-repellent activity, but typically have a relatively short duration of action.

ILLUSTRATION BY PHOTOTAKE.

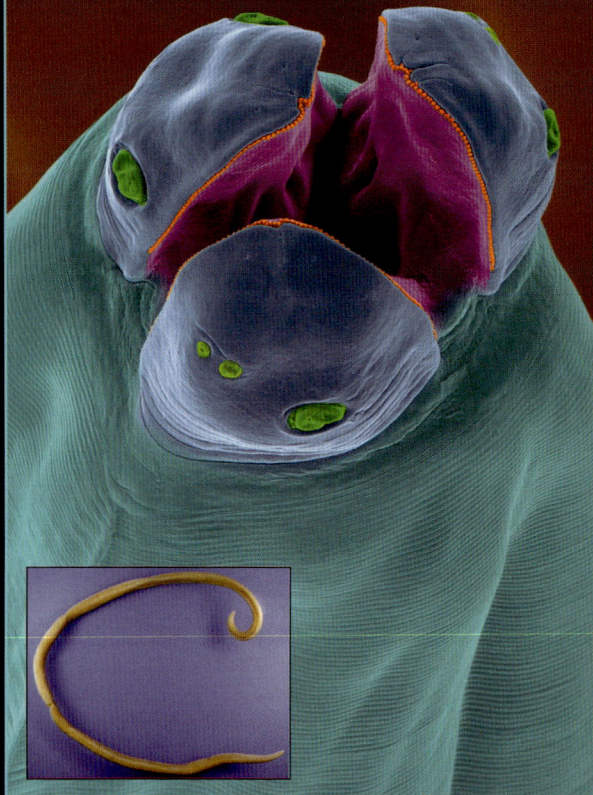

The image caption on the SEM photo reads vertically: S. E. M. BY DR. DENNIS KUNKEL, UNIVERSITY OF HAWAII. INSET BY TAM C. NGUYEN.

The ascarid roundworm *Toxocara canis,* showing the mouth with three lips. INSET: Photomicrograph of the roundworm *Ascaris lumbricoides.*

# INTERNAL PARASITES: WORMS

## ASCARIDS

Ascarids are intestinal round-worms that rarely cause severe disease in dogs. Nonetheless, they are of major public health signifi-cance because they can be trans-ferred to people. Sadly, it is chil-dren who are most commonly affected by the parasite, probably from inadvertently ingesting ascarid-contaminated soil. In fact, many yards and children's sand-boxes contain appreciable numbers of ascarid eggs. So, while ascarids don't bite dogs or latch onto their intestines to suck blood, they do cause some nasty medical conditions in children and are best eradicated from our furry friends. Because pups can start passing ascarid eggs by three weeks of age, most parasite-control programs begin at two weeks of age and are repeated every two weeks until pups are eight weeks old. It is important to

S. E. M. BY DR. DENNIS KUNKEL, UNIVERSITY OF HAWAII.

realize that bitches can pass ascarids to their pups even if they test negative prior to whelping. Accordingly, bitches are best treated at the same time as the pups.

### HOOKWORMS

Unlike ascarids, hookworms do latch onto a dog's intestinal tract and can cause significant loss of blood and protein. Similar to ascarids, hookworms can be transmitted to humans, where they cause a condition known as cutaneous larval migrans. Dogs can become infected either by consuming the infective larvae or by the larvae's penetrating the skin directly. People most often get infected when they are lying on the ground (such as on a beach) and the larvae penetrate the skin. Yes, the larvae can penetrate through a beach blanket. Hookworms are typically susceptible to the same medications used to treat ascarids.

**The hookworm *Ancylostoma caninum* infests the intestines of dogs. INSET: Note the row of hooks at the posterior end, used to anchor the worm to the intestinal wall.**

**WHIPWORMS**

Whipworms latch onto the lower aspects of the dog's colon and can cause cramping and diarrhea. Eggs do not start to appear in the dog's feces until about three months after the dog was infected. This worm has a peculiar life cycle, which makes it more difficult to control than ascarids or hookworms. The good thing is that whipworms rarely are transferred to people.

Some of the medications used to treat ascarids and hookworms are also effective against whipworms, but, in general, a separate treatment protocol is needed. Since most of the medications are effective against the adults but not the eggs or larvae, treatment is typically repeated in three weeks, and then often in three

Adult whipworm, *Trichuris* sp., an intestinal parasite.

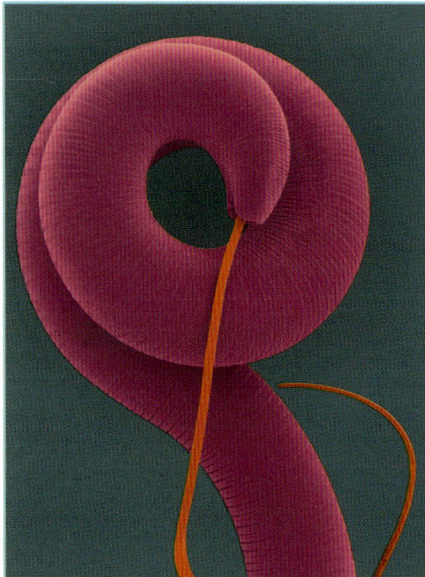

S. E. M. BY DR. DENNIS KUNKEL, UNIVERSITY OF HAWAII

**WORM-CONTROL GUIDELINES**
- Practice sanitary habits with your dog and home.
- Clean up after your dog and don't let him sniff or eat other dogs' droppings.
- Control insects and fleas in the dog's environment. Fleas, lice, cockroaches, beetles, mice and rats can act as hosts for various worms.
- Prevent dogs from eating uncooked meat, raw poultry and dead animals.
- Keep dogs and children from playing in sand and soil.
- Kennel dogs on cement or gravel; avoid dirt runs.
- Administer heartworm preventives regularly.
- Have your vet examine your dog's stools at your annual visits.
- Select a boarding kennel carefully so as to avoid contamination from other dogs or an unsanitary environment.
- Prevent dogs from roaming. Obey local leash laws.

months as well. Unfortunately, since dogs don't develop resistance to whipworms, it is difficult to prevent them from getting reinfected if they visit soil contaminated with whipworm eggs.

**TAPEWORMS**

There are many different species of tapeworm that affect dogs, but *Dipylidium caninum* is probably the most common and is spread by fleas. Flea larvae feed on organic debris and tapeworm eggs in the environment and, when a dog chews at himself and manages to ingest fleas, he might get a dose of tapeworm at the same time. The tapeworm then develops further in the intestine of the dog.

The tapeworm itself, which is a parasitic flatworm that latches onto the intestinal wall, is composed of numerous segments. When the segments break off into the intestine (as proglottids), they may accumulate around the rectum like grains of rice. While this tapeworm is disgusting in its behavior, it is not directly communicable to humans (although humans can also get infected by swallowing fleas).

A much more dangerous flatworm is *Echinococcus multilocularis*, which is typically found in foxes, coyotes and wolves. The eggs are passed in the feces and infect rodents, and, when dogs eat the rodents, the dogs can be infected by thousands of adult tapeworms. While the parasites don't cause many problems in dogs, this is considered the most lethal worm infection that people can get. Take appropriate precautions if you live in an area in which these tapeworms are found. Do not use mulch that may contain feces of dogs, cats or wildlife, and discourage your pets from hunting

wildlife. Treat these tapeworm infections aggressively in pets, because if humans get infected, approximately half die.

## HEARTWORMS

Heartworm disease is caused by the parasite *Dirofilaria immitis* and is seen in dogs around the world. A member of the roundworm group, it is spread between dogs by the bite of an infected mosquito. The mosquito injects infective larvae into the dog's skin with its bite, and these larvae develop under the skin for a period of time before making their way to the heart. There they develop into adults, which grow and create blockages of the heart, lungs and major blood vessels there. They also start producing offspring (microfilariae)

S. E. M. by Dr. Dennis Kunkel, University of Hawaii.

A dog tapeworm proglottid (body segment).

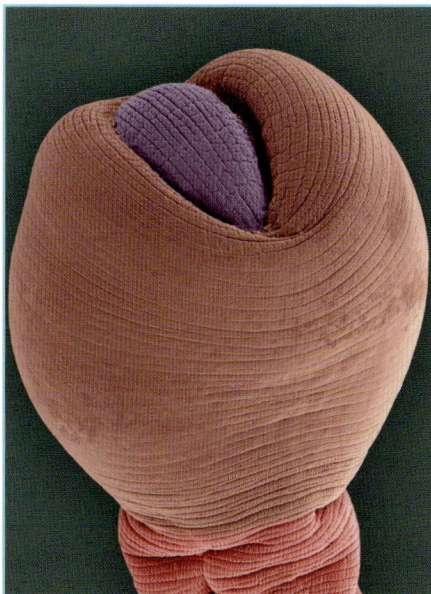
S. E. M. by Dr. Dennis Kunkel, University of Hawaii.

The dog tapeworm *Taenia pisiformis.*

## A Look at Internal Parasites

PHOTO BY CAROLINA BIOLOGICAL SUPPLY CO.

Ascarid *Rhabditis*

PHOTO BY CAROLINA BIOLOGICAL SUPPLY CO.

Hookworm *Ancylostoma caninum*

PHOTO BY TAM C. NGUYEN.

Tapeworm *Dipylidium caninum*

PHOTO BY TAM C. NGUYEN.

Heartworm *Dirofilaria immitis*

and these microfilariae circulate in the bloodstream, waiting to hitch a ride when the next mosquito bites. Once in the mosquito, the microfilariae develop into infective larvae and the entire process is repeated.

When dogs get infected with heartworm, over time they tend to develop symptoms associated with heart disease, such as coughing, exercise intolerance and potentially many other manifestations. Diagnosis is confirmed by either seeing the microfilariae themselves in blood samples or using immunologic tests (antigen testing) to identify the presence of adult heartworms. Since antigen tests measure the presence of adult heartworms and microfilarial tests measure offspring produced by adults, neither are positive until six to seven months after the initial infection. However, the beginning of damage can occur by fifth-stage larvae as early as three months after infection. Thus it is possible for dogs to be harboring problem-causing larvae for up to three months before either type of test would identify an infection.

The good news is that there are great protocols available for preventing heartworm in dogs. Testing is critical in the process, and it is important to understand the benefits as well as the limitations of such testing. All dogs six months of age or older that have not been on continuous heartworm-preventive medication should be

## Life Cycle of the Heartworm

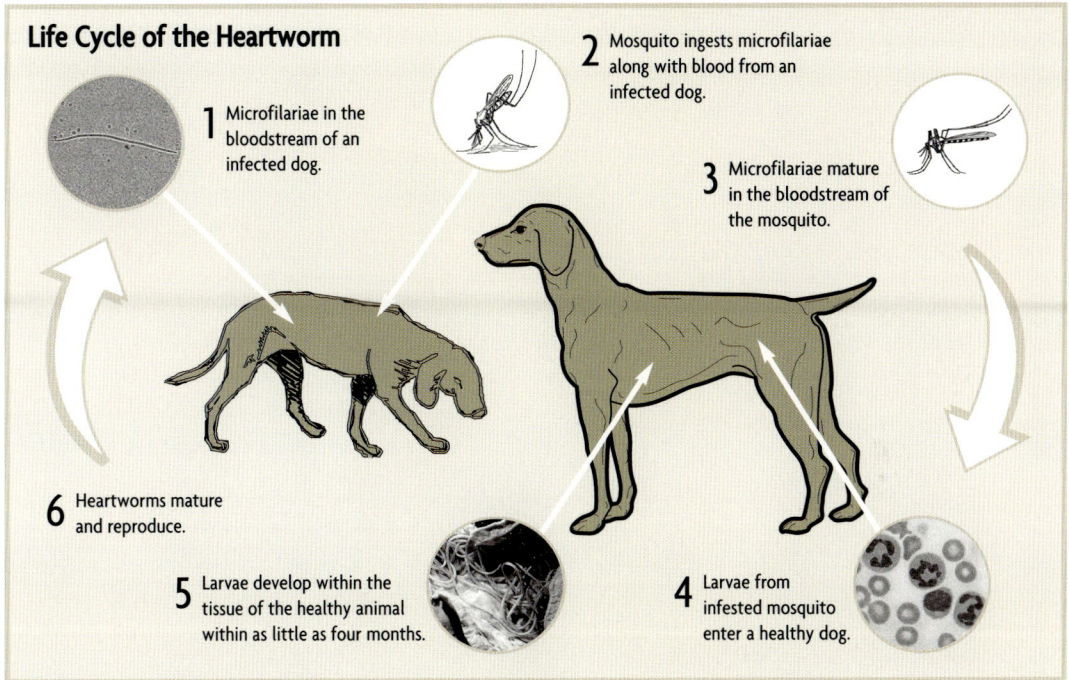

1 Microfilariae in the bloodstream of an infected dog.

2 Mosquito ingests microfilariae along with blood from an infected dog.

3 Microfilariae mature in the bloodstream of the mosquito.

4 Larvae from infested mosquito enter a healthy dog.

5 Larvae develop within the tissue of the healthy animal within as little as four months.

6 Heartworms mature and reproduce.

screened with microfilarial or antigen tests. For dogs receiving preventive medication, periodic antigen testing helps assess the effectiveness of the preventives. The American Heartworm Society guidelines suggest that annual retesting may not be necessary when owners have absolutely provided continuous heartworm prevention. Retesting on a two- to three-year interval may be sufficient in these cases. However, your veterinarian will likely have specific guidelines under which heartworm preventives will be prescribed, and many prefer to err on the side of safety and retest annually.

It is indeed fortunate that heartworm is relatively easy to prevent, because treatments can be as life-threatening as the disease itself. Treatment requires a two-step process that kills the adult heartworms first and then the microfilariae. Prevention is obviously preferable; this involves a once-monthly oral or topical treatment. The most common oral preventives include ivermectin (not suitable for some breeds), moxidectin and milbemycin oxime; the once-a-month topical drug selamectin provides heartworm protection in addition to flea, tick and other parasite controls.

# Number-One Killer Disease in Dogs: CANCER

In every age, there is a word associated with a disease or plague that causes humans to shudder. In the 21st century, that word is "cancer." Just as cancer is the leading cause of death in humans, it claims nearly half the lives of dogs that die from a natural disease as well as half the dogs that die over the age of ten years.

Described as a genetic disease, cancer becomes a greater risk as the dog ages. Vets and dog owners have become increasingly aware of the threat of cancer to dogs. Statistics reveal that one dog in every five will develop cancer, the most common of which is skin cancer. Many cancers, including prostate, ovarian and breast cancer, can be avoided by spaying and neutering our dogs by the age of six months.

Early detection of cancer can save or extend a dog's life, so it is absolutely vital for owners to have their dogs examined by a qualified vet or oncologist immediately upon detection of any abnormality. Certain dietary guidelines have also proven to reduce the onset and spread of cancer. Foods based on fish rather than beef, due to the presence of Omega-3 fatty acids, are recommended. Other amino acids such as glutamine have significant benefits for canines, particularly those breeds that show a greater susceptibility to cancer.

Cancer management and treatments promise hope for future generations of canines. Since the disease is genetic, breeders should never breed a dog whose parents, grandparents and any related siblings have developed cancer. It is difficult to know whether to exclude an otherwise healthy dog from a breeding program, as the disease does not manifest itself until the dog's senior years.

## RECOGNIZE CANCER WARNING SIGNS

Since early detection can possibly rescue your dog from becoming a cancer statistic, it is essential for owners to recognize the possible signs and seek the assistance of a qualified professional.

- Abnormal bumps or lumps that continue to grow
- Bleeding or discharge from any body cavity
- Persistent stiffness or lameness
- Recurrent sores or sores that do not heal
- Inappetence
- Breathing difficulties
- Weight loss
- Bad breath or odors
- General malaise and fatigue
- Eating and swallowing problems
- Difficulty urinating and defecating

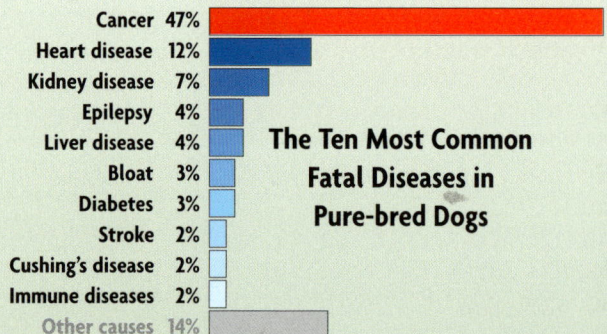

| Disease | Percentage |
|---|---|
| Cancer | 47% |
| Heart disease | 12% |
| Kidney disease | 7% |
| Epilepsy | 4% |
| Liver disease | 4% |
| Bloat | 3% |
| Diabetes | 3% |
| Stroke | 2% |
| Cushing's disease | 2% |
| Immune diseases | 2% |
| Other causes | 14% |

**The Ten Most Common Fatal Diseases in Pure-bred Dogs**

# SCOTTISH DEERHOUND

**WHEN IS MY DOG A "SENIOR"?**
In general, pure-bred dogs are considered to have achieved senior status when they reach 75% of their breed's average lifespan, with breed size having some bearing on the expected lifespan. Your Scottish Deerhound has an average lifespan of around ten years and thus is a senior citizen at around seven.

Obviously, the old "seven dog years to one human year" theory is not exact. In puppyhood, a dog's year is actually comparable to more than seven human years, considering the puppy's rapid growth during his first year. Then, in adulthood, the ratio decreases. Regardless, the more viable rule of thumb is that the larger the dog, the shorter his expected lifespan. Of course, this can vary among individual dogs, with many living longer than expected, which we hope is the case!

**WHAT ARE THE SIGNS OF AGING?**
By the time your dog has reached his senior years, you will know him very well, so the physical and behavioral changes that accompany aging should be noticeable to you.

Humans and dogs share the most obvious physical sign of aging: gray hair! Graying often occurs first on the muzzle and face, around the eyes. Other telltale signs are the dog's overall decrease in activity. Your older dog might be more content to nap and rest, and he may not show the same old enthusiasm when it's time to play in the yard or go for a walk. Other physical signs include significant weight loss or gain; more labored movement; skin and coat problems, possibly hair loss; sight

**WEATHER WORRIES**
Older pets are less tolerant of extremes in weather, both heat and cold. Your older dog should not spend extended periods in the sun; when outdoors in the warm weather, make sure he does not become overheated. In chilly weather, consider a sweater for your dog when outdoors and limit time spent outside. Whether or not his coat is thinning, he will need provisions to keep him warm when the weather is cold. You may even place his bed by a heating duct in your living room or bedroom.

A senior Scottish Deerhound still looking happy, healthy and in good condition.

and/or hearing problems; changes in toileting habits, perhaps seeming "unhousebroken" at times; and tooth decay, bad breath or other mouth problems.

There are behavioral changes that go along with aging, too. There are numerous causes for behavioral changes. Sometimes a dog's apparent confusion results from a physical change like diminished sight or hearing. If his confusion causes him to be afraid, he may act aggressively or defensively. He may sleep more frequently because his daily walks, though shorter now, tire him out. He may begin to experience separation anxiety or, conversely, become less interested in petting and attention.

There also are clinical conditions that cause behavioral changes in older dogs. One such condition is known as canine cognitive dysfunction (familiarly known as "old-dog" syndrome). It can be frustrating for an owner whose dog is affected with cognitive dysfunction, as it can result in behavioral changes of all types, most seemingly unexplainable. Common changes include the dog's forgetting aspects of the daily routine, such as times to eat, going out for walks, relieving himself and the like. Along the same lines, you may take your dog out at the regular time for a potty trip and he may have no idea why he is there. Sometimes a placid dog will begin to show aggressive or possessive tendencies or, conversely, a hyperactive dog will start to "mellow out."

Disease also can be the cause of behavioral changes in senior dogs. Hormonal problems (Cushing's disease is common in older dogs), diabetes and thyroid disease can cause increased appetite, which can lead to aggression related to food guarding. It's better to be proactive with your senior dog, making more frequent trips to the vet if necessary and having bloodwork done to test for the diseases that can commonly befall older dogs.

This is not to say that, as dogs age, they all fall apart physically and become nasty in personality. The aforementioned changes are discussed to alert owners to the things that may happen as their dogs get older. Many hardy dogs remain active and alert well into

**ACCIDENT ALERT!**
Just as we puppy-proof our homes for the new member of the family, we must accident-proof our homes for the older dog. You want to create a safe environment in which the senior dog can get around easily and comfortably, with no dangers. A dog that slips and falls in old age is much more prone to injury than an adult, making accident prevention even more important. Likewise, dogs are more prone to falls in old age, as they do not have the same balance and coordination that they once had. Diminished sight and hearing can make it harder to get around, too. Throw rugs on hardwood floors are slippery and pose a risk; even a throw rug on a carpeted surface can be an obstacle for the senior dog. Consider putting down non-slip surfaces or confining your dog to carpeted rooms only.

might reach the estimated "senior" age for the breed and show no signs of slowing down. However, even if he shows no outward signs of aging, he should begin a senior-care program once he reaches the determined age. He may not show it, but he's not a pup anymore! By providing him with extra attention to his veterinary care at this age, you will be practicing good preventive medicine, ensuring that the rest of your dog's life will be as long, active, happy and healthy as possible. If you do notice indications of aging, such as graying and/or changes in sleeping, eating or toileting habits, this is a sign to set up a senior-care visit with your vet right away to make sure that these changes are not related to any health problems.

To start, senior dogs should visit the vet twice yearly for exams, routine tests and overall evaluations. Many veterinarians have special screening programs

old age. However, it can be frustrating and heartbreaking for owners to see their beloved dogs change physically and temperamentally. Just know that it's the same Scottish Deerhound under there, and that he still loves you and appreciates your care, which he needs now more than ever.

**HOW DO I CARE FOR MY AGING DOG?**
Again, every dog is an individual in terms of aging. Your Deerhound

Some dogs never lose their curiosity, even as seniors! This senior inspects the landscaping.

especially for senior dogs that can include a thorough physical exam; blood test to determine complete blood count; serum biochemistry test, which screens for liver, kidney and blood problems as well as cancer; urinalysis; and dental exams. With these tests, it can be determined whether your dog has any health problems; the results also establish a baseline for your pet against which future test results can be compared.

In addition to these tests, your vet may suggest additional testing, including an EKG, tests for glaucoma and other problems of the eye, chest x-rays, screening for tumors, blood pressure test, test for thyroid function and screening for parasites and reassessment of his preventive program. Your vet also will ask you questions about your dog's diet and activity level, what you feed and the amounts that you feed. This information, along with his evaluation of the dog's overall condition, will enable him to suggest proper dietary changes, if needed.

This may seem like quite a work-up for your pet, but veterinarians advise that older dogs need more frequent attention so that any health problems can be detected as early as possible. Serious conditions like kidney disease, heart disease and cancer may not present outward symptoms, or the problem may go undetected if the symptoms are mistaken by owners as just part of the aging process.

There are some conditions more common in elderly dogs that are difficult to ignore. Cognitive dysfunction shares much in common with senility and Alzheimer's disease, and dogs are not immune. Dogs can become confused and/or disoriented, lose their house-training, have abnormal sleep-wake cycles and interact differently with their owners. Be heartened by the fact that, in some ways, there are more treatment options for dogs with cognitive dysfunction than for people with similar conditions. There is good evidence that continued stimulation in the form of games, play, training and exercise can help to maintain cognitive function. There are also medications (such as seligiline) and antioxidant-fortified senior diets that have been shown to be beneficial.

Cancer is also a condition more common in the elderly. Although lung cancer, which is a major killer in humans, is relatively rare in dogs, almost all other cancers seen in people are also seen in pets. If pets are getting regular physical examinations, cancers are often detected early. There are a variety of cancer therapies available today, and many pets continue to live happy lives with appropriate treatment.

Degenerative joint disease, often referred to as arthritis, is another malady common to both elderly dogs and humans. A lifetime of wear and tear on joints and running around at play eventually takes its toll and results in stiffness and difficulty in getting around. As dogs live longer and healthier lives, it is natural that they should eventually feel some of the effects of aging. Once again, if regular veterinary care has been available, your pet should not have been carrying extra pounds all those years and wearing those joints out before their time. If your pet was unfortunate enough to inherit hip dysplasia, osteochondritis dissecans or any of the other developmental orthopedic diseases, battling the onset of degenerative joint disease was probably a longstanding goal. In any case, there are now many effective remedies for managing degenerative joint disease and a number of remarkable surgeries as well.

Aside from the extra veterinary care, there is much you can do at home to keep your older dog in good condition. The dog's diet is an important factor. If your dog's appetite decreases, he will not be getting the nutrients he needs. He also will lose weight, which is unhealthy for a dog at a proper weight. Conversely, an older dog's metabolism is slower and he usually exercises less, but he should not be allowed to become obese. Obesity in an older dog is especially risky, because extra pounds mean extra stress on the body, increasing his vulnerability to heart disease. Additionally, the extra pounds make it harder for the dog to move about.

You should discuss age-related feeding changes with your vet. For a dog who has lost interest in food, it may be suggested to try some different types of food until you find something new that the dog likes. For an obese dog, a "light"-formula dog food or reducing food portions may be advised, along with exercise appropriate to his physical condition and energy level.

As for exercise, the senior dog should not be allowed to become a "couch potato" despite his old age. He may not be able to handle the morning run, long walks and vigorous games of fetch, but he still needs to get up and get moving. Keep up with your daily

### GDV IN OLDER DOGS

We already know that bloat (gastric dilatation/volvulus) commonly affects deep-chested dogs of all ages. Furthermore, studies indicate that dogs who are over seven years of age are twice as prone to the condition as young dogs half their age. Be extra-conscious about practicing the bloat preventives you've always incorporated into your dog's routine.

walks, but keep the distances shorter and let your dog set the pace. If he gets to the point where he's not up for walks, let him stroll around the yard. On the other hand, many dogs remain very active in their senior years, so base changes to the exercise program on your own individual dog and what he's capable of. Don't worry, your Scottish Deerhound will let you know when it's time to rest.

Keep up with your grooming routine as you always have. Be extra-diligent about checking the skin and coat for problems. Older dogs can experience thinning coats as a normal aging process, but they can also lose hair as a result of medical problems. Some thinning is normal, but patches of baldness or the loss of significant amounts of hair is not.

Hopefully, you've been regular with brushing your dog's teeth

## AH, MY ACHING BONES!

As your pet ages and things that once were routine become difficult for him to handle, you may need to make some adjustments around the home to make things easier for your dog. Senior dogs affected by arthritis may have trouble moving about. If you notice this in your dog, you may have to limit him to one floor of the house so that he does not have to deal with stairs. If there are a few steps leading out into the yard, a ramp may help the dog. Likewise, he may need a ramp or a boost to get in and out of the car. Ensure that he has plenty of soft bedding on which to sleep and rest, as this will be comfortable for his aching joints. Also ensure that surfaces on which the dog walks are not slippery.

Investigate new dietary supplements made for arthritic dogs. Studies have found that products containing glucosamine added once or twice daily to the senior dog's food can have beneficial effects on the dog's joints. Many of these products also contain natural anti-inflammatories such as chondroitin, MSM and cetyl myristoleate, as well as natural herbal remedies and nutmeg. Talk to your vet about these supplements.

A good remedy for an aching dog is to give him a gentle massage each day, or even a few times a day if possible. This can be especially beneficial before your dog gets out of his bed in the morning. Just as in humans, massage can decrease pain in dogs whether the dog is arthritic or just afflicted by the stiffness that accompanies old age. Gently massage his joints and limbs, and pet him on his entire body. This can help his circulation and flexibility and ease any joint or muscle aches. Massaging your dog has benefits for you, too; in fact, just petting our dogs can cause reduced levels of stress and lower our blood pressure. Massage and petting also help you find any previously undetected lumps, bumps or abnormalities. Often these are not visible and only turn up by being felt.

throughout his life. Healthy teeth directly affect overall good health. We already know that bacteria from gum infections can enter the dog's body through the damaged gums and travel to the organs. At a stage in life when his organs don't function as well as they used to, you don't want anything to put additional strain on them. Clean teeth also contribute to a healthy immune system. Offering the dental-type chews in addition to toothbrushing can help, as they remove plaque and tartar as the dog chews.

Along with the same good care you've given him all of his life, pay a little extra attention to your dog in his senior years and keep up with twice-yearly trips to the vet. The sooner a problem is uncovered, the greater the chances of a full recovery.

## SAYING GOODBYE

While you can help your dog live as long a life as possible, you can't help him live forever. A dog's lifespan is short when compared to that of a human, so it is inevitable that pet owners will experience loss. To many, losing a beloved dog is like losing a family member. Our dogs are part of our lives every day; they are our true loyal friends and always seem to know when it's time to comfort us, to celebrate with us or to just provide the company of a caring friend. Even when we know that

our dog is nearing his final days, we can never quite prepare for his being gone.

Many dogs live out long lives and simply die of old age. Others unfortunately are taken suddenly by illness or accident, and still others find their senior years compromised by disease and physical problems. In some of these cases, owners find themselves having to make difficult decisions.

### MEMORIALIZING YOUR PET

Whether and how you choose to memorialize your pet is completely up to you. Some owners feel that this helps their healing process by allowing them some closure. Likewise, some owners feel that memorialization is a meaningful way to acknowledge their departed pets. Some owners opt to bury their deceased pets in their own yards, using special stones, flowers or trees to mark the sites. Others opt for the services of a pet cemetery, in which many of the privileges available for humans, such as funeral and viewing services, caskets and gravestones, are available for pets. Cremation is an option, either individual or communal. Owners then can opt to have their dogs' ashes buried, scattered or kept in an urn as a memorial. Your vet will likely know of the services available in your locality and can help you make arrangements if you choose one of these options.

# SCOTTISH DEERHOUND

Is dog showing in your blood? Are you excited by the idea of gaiting your handsome Scottish Deerhound around the ring to the thunderous applause of an enthusiastic audience? Are you certain that your beloved Scottish Deerhound is flawless? You are not alone! Every loving owner thinks that his dog has no faults, or too few to mention. No matter how many times an owner reads the breed standard, he cannot find any faults in his aristocratic companion dog. If this sounds like you, and if you are considering entering your Scottish Deerhound in a dog show, here are some basic questions to ask yourself:

• Did you purchase a "show-quality" puppy from the breeder?
• Is your puppy at least six months of age?
• Does the puppy exhibit correct show type for his breed?
• Does your puppy have any disqualifying faults?
• Is your Scottish Deerhound registered with the American Kennel Club?
• How much time do you have to devote to training, grooming, conditioning and exhibiting your dog?

• Do you understand the rules and regulations of a dog show?
• Do you have time to learn how to show your dog properly?
• Do you have the financial resources to invest in showing your dog?
• Will you show the dog yourself or hire a professional handler?
• Do you have a vehicle that can accommodate your weekend trips to the dog shows?

Success in the show ring requires more than a pretty face, a waggy tail and a pocketful of liver. Even though dog shows can be exciting and enjoyable, the sport of conformation makes great demands on the exhibitors and the dogs. Winning exhibitors live for their dogs, devoting time and money to their dogs' presentation, conditioning and training. Very few novices, even those with good

**AKC GROUPS**
For showing purposes, the American Kennel Club divides its recognized breeds into seven groups: Hounds, Sporting Dogs, Working Dogs, Terriers, Toys, Non-Sporting Dogs and Herding Dogs.

dogs, will find themselves in the winners' circle, though it does happen. Don't be disheartened, though. Every exhibitor began as a novice and worked his way up to the Group ring. It's the "working your way up" part that you must keep in mind.

Assuming that you have purchased a puppy of the correct type and quality for showing, let's begin to examine the world of showing and what's required to get started. Although the entry fee into a dog show is nominal, there are lots of other hidden costs involved with "finishing" your Scottish Deerhound, that is, making him a champion. Things like equipment, travel, training and conditioning all cost money. A more serious campaign will include fees for a professional handler, boarding, cross-country travel and advertising. Top-winning show dogs can represent a very considerable investment—over $100,000 has been spent in campaigning some dogs. (The investment can be less, of course, for owners who don't use professional handlers.)

Many owners, on the other hand, enter their "average" Scottish Deerhounds in dog shows for the fun and enjoyment of it. Dog showing makes an absorbing hobby, with many rewards for dogs and owners alike. If you're having fun, meeting other people who share your interests and enjoying the overall experience, you likely will catch the "bug." Once the dog-

Dogs in the show ring are "stacked," meaning that they stand in a position to show them off to their best advantage.

show bug bites, its effects can last a lifetime; it's certainly much better than a deer tick! Soon you will be envisioning yourself in the center ring at the Westminster Kennel Club Dog Show in New York City, competing for the prestigious Best in Show cup. This magical dog show is televised annually from Madison Square Garden, and the victorious dog becomes a celebrity overnight.

**AKC CONFORMATION BASICS**

Visiting a dog show as a spectator is a great place to start. Pick up the show catalog to find out what time your breed is being shown, who is judging the breed and in which ring the classes will be held. To start, Scottish Deerhounds compete against other Scottish Deerhounds, and the winner is selected as Best of Breed by the judge. This is the procedure for each breed. At a group show, all of the Best of Breed winners go on to compete for Group One (first place) in their respective group. For example, all

**FIVE CLASSES AT SHOWS**

At most AKC all-breed shows, there are five regular classes offered: Puppy, Novice, Bred-by-Exhibitor, American-bred and Open. The Puppy Class is usually divided as 6 to 9 months of age and 9 to 12 months of age. When deciding in which class to enter your dog, whether male or female, you must carefully check the show schedule to make sure that you have selected the right class. Depending on the age of the dog, previous first-place wins and the sex of the dog, you must make the best choice. It is possible to enter a one-year-old dog who has not won sufficient first places in any of the non-Puppy Classes, though the competition is more intense the further you progress from the Puppy Class.

Best of Breed winners in a given group compete against each other; this is done for all seven groups. Finally, all seven group winners go head to head in the ring for the Best in Show award.

An interesting class is the brace class, in which nearly identical dogs compete in pairs. These braces and their handlers take a turn around the ring for the judge.

The judge reviews the line of Scottish Deerhounds, examining each dog individually. As well as looking at each dog's overall appearance, in relation to the breed standard, she feels for correct bone structure.

What most spectators don't understand is the basic idea of conformation. A dog show is often referred as a "conformation" show. This means that the judge should decide how each dog stacks up (conforms) to the breed standard for his given breed: how well does this Scottish Deerhound conform to the ideal representative detailed in the standard? Ideally, this is what happens. In reality, however, this ideal often gets slighted as the judge compares Scottish Deerhound #1 to Scottish Deerhound #2. Again, the ideal is that each dog is judged based on his merits in comparison to his breed standard, not in comparison to the other dogs in the ring. It is easier for judges to compare dogs of the same breed to decide which they think is the better specimen; in the Group and Best in Show ring, however, it is very difficult to compare one breed to another, like apples to oranges. Thus the dog's conformation to the breed standard—not to mention advertising dollars and good handling—is essential to success in conformation shows. The dog described in the standard (the standard for each AKC breed is written and approved by the breed's national parent club

## BECOMING A CHAMPION

An official AKC championship of record requires that a dog accumulate 15 points under three different judges, including two "majors" under different judges. Points are awarded based on the number of dogs entered into competition, varying from breed to breed and place to place. A win of three, four or five points is considered a "major." The AKC annually assigns a schedule of points to adjust for variations that accompany a breed's popularity and the population of a given area.

and then submitted to the AKC for approval) is the perfect dog of that breed, and breeders keep their eye on the standard when they choose which dogs to breed, hoping to get closer and closer to the ideal with each litter.

Another good first step for the novice is to join a dog club. You will be astonished by the many and different kinds of dog clubs in the country, with about 5,000 clubs holding events every year. Most clubs require that prospective new members present two letters of recommendation from existing members. Perhaps you've made some friends visiting a show held by a particular club and you would like to join that club. Dog clubs may specialize in a single breed, like a local or regional Scottish Deerhound club, or in a specific pursuit, such as obedience, tracking or lure-coursing events. There are all-breed clubs for all dog enthusiasts; they sponsor special training days, seminars on topics like grooming or handling or lectures on breeding or canine genetics. There are also clubs that specialize in certain types of dogs, like sighthounds, hunting dogs, companion dogs, etc.

A parent club is the national organization, sanctioned by the AKC, which promotes and safeguards its breed in the country. The Scottish Deerhound Club of America can be contacted on the Internet at www.deerhound.org.

**OTHER TYPES OF COMPETITION**
In addition to conformation shows, the AKC holds a variety of other competitive events. Obedience trials, agility trials and tracking trials are open to all breeds, while hunting tests, field trials, lure coursing, herding tests and trials, earthdog tests and coonhound events are limited to specific breeds or groups of breeds. The Junior Showmanship program is offered to aspiring young handlers and their dogs, and the Canine Good Citizen® Program is an all-around good-behavior test open to all dogs, pure-bred and mixed.

The parent club holds an annual national specialty show, usually in a different city each year, in which many of the country's top dogs, handlers and breeders gather to compete. At a specialty show, only members of a single breed are invited to participate. There are also group specialties, in which all members of a group are invited. For more information about dog clubs in your area, contact the AKC at www.akc.org on the Internet or write them at their Raleigh, NC address.

**OBEDIENCE TRIALS**
Mrs. Helen Whitehouse Walker, a Standard Poodle fancier, can be credited with introducing obedience trials to the United

Whether or not you go home a winner, showing should be an enjoyable activity for all participants, human and canine.

States. In the 1930s she designed a series of exercises based on those of the Associated Sheep, Police, Army Dog Society of Great Britain. These exercises were intended to evaluate the working relationship between dog and owner. Since those early days of the sport in the US, obedience trials have grown more and more popular, and now more than 2,000 trials each year attract over 100,000 dogs and their owners. Any dog registered with the AKC, regardless of neutering or other disqualifications that would preclude entry in conformation competition, can participate in obedience trials.

There are three levels of difficulty in obedience competition. The first (and easiest) level is the Novice, in which dogs can earn the Companion Dog (CD) title. The intermediate level is the Open level, in which the Companion Dog Excellent (CDX) title is awarded. The advanced level is the Utility level, in which dogs compete for the Utility Dog (UD) title. Classes at each level are further divided into "A" and "B," with "A" for beginners and "B" for those with more experience. In order to win a title at a given level, a dog must earn three "legs." A "leg" is accomplished when a dog scores 170 or higher (200 is a perfect score). The scoring system gets a little trickier when you understand that a dog must score more than 50% of the points available for each exercise in order to actually earn the points. Available points for each exercise range between 20 and 40.

Once he's earned the UD title, a dog can go on to win the prestigious title of Utility Dog Excellent

(UDX) by winning "legs" in ten shows. Additionally, Utility Dogs who win "legs" in Open B and Utility B earn points toward the lofty title of Obedience Trial Champion (OTCh.). Established in 1977 by the AKC, this title requires a dog to earn 100 points as well as three first places in a combination of Open B and Utility B classes under three different judges. The "brass ring" of obedience competition is the AKC's National Obedience Invitational. This is an exclusive competition for only the cream of the obedience crop. In order to qualify for the invitational, a dog must be ranked in either the top 25 all-breeds in obedience or in the top three for

**TRACKING**

Tracking tests are exciting ways to test your Scottish Deerhound's instinctive scenting ability on a competitive level. All dogs have a nose, and all breeds are welcome in tracking tests. The first AKC-licensed tracking test took place in 1937 as part of the Utility level at an obedience trial, and thus competitive tracking was officially begun. The first title, Tracking Dog (TD), was offered in 1947, ten years after the first official tracking test. It was not until 1980 that the AKC added the title Tracking Dog Excellent (TDX), which was followed by the title Versatile Surface Tracking (VST) in 1995. Champion Tracker (CT) is awarded to a dog who has earned all three of those titles.

his breed in obedience. The title at stake here is that of National Obedience Champion (NOC).

**AGILITY TRIALS**

Agility trials became sanctioned by the AKC in August 1994, when the first licensed agility trials were held. Since that time, agility certainly has grown in popularity by leaps and bounds, literally! The AKC allows all registered breeds (including Miscellaneous Class breeds) to participate, providing the dog is 12 months of age or older. Agility is designed so that the handler demonstrates how well the dog can work at his side. The handler directs his dog through, over, under and around an obstacle course that includes jumps, tires, the dog walk, weave poles, pipe tunnels, collapsed tunnels and more. While working his way through the course, the dog must keep one eye and ear on the handler and the rest of his body on the course. The handler runs along with the dog, giving verbal and hand signals to guide the dog through the course.

The first organization to promote agility trials in the US was the United States Dog Agility Association, Inc. (USDAA). Established in 1986, the USDAA sparked the formation of many member clubs around the country. To participate in USDAA trials, dogs must be at least 18 months of age. The USDAA and AKC both offer titles to winning dogs, although the exercises and requirements of the two organizations differ.

Agility trials are a great way to keep your dog active, and they will keep you running, too! You should join a local agility club to learn more about the sport. These clubs offer sessions in which you can introduce your dog to the various obstacles as well as training classes to prepare him for competition. In no time, your dog will be climbing A-frames, crossing the dog walk and flying over hurdles, all with you right beside him. Your heart will leap every time your dog jumps through the hoop—and you'll be having just as much (if not more) fun!

## LURE COURSING

Owners of sighthound breeds have the opportunity to participate in lure coursing with their dogs. Lure-coursing events are exciting and fast-paced, requiring dogs to follow an artificial lure around a course on an open field. Scores are based on the dog's speed, enthusiasm, agility, endurance and ability to follow the lure. At the non-competitive level, lure coursing is designed to gauge a sighthound's instinctive coursing ability. Competitive lure coursing is more demanding, requiring training and conditioning for a dog to develop his coursing instincts and skills to the fullest, thus preserving the intended function of all sighthound breeds. Breeds eligible for AKC lure coursing are the Scottish Deerhound, Whippet, Basenji, Greyhound, Italian Greyhound, Afghan Hound, Borzoi, Ibizan Hound, Pharaoh Hound, Irish

In a lure-coursing event, the handlers "slip" the dogs to begin the stake.

Wolfhound, Saluki and Rhodesian Ridgeback.

Lure coursing on a competitive level is certainly wonderful physical and mental exercise for a dog. A dog must be at least one year of age to enter an AKC coursing event, and he must not have any disqualifications according to his breed standard. Check the AKC's rules and regulations for details. To get started, you can consult the AKC's website to help you find a coursing club in your area. A club can introduce you to the sport and help you learn how to train your dog correctly.

Titles awarded in lure coursing are Junior Courser (JC), Senior Courser (SC) and Master Courser (MC); these are suffix titles, affixed to the end of the dog's name. The Field Champion (FC) title is a prefix title affixed to the beginning of the dog's name. A Dual Champion is a hound that

has earned both a Field Champion title as well as a show championship. A Triple Champion (TC) title is awarded to a dog that is a Champion, Field Champion and Obedience Trial Champion. The suffix Lure Courser Excellent (LCX) is given to a dog who has earned the FC title plus 45 additional championship points, and number designations are added to the title upon each additional 45 championship points earned (LCX II, III, IV and so on).

Sighthounds also can participate in events sponsored by the American Sighthound Field Association (ASFA), an organization devoted to the pursuit of lure coursing. The ASFA was founded in 1972 as a means of keeping open field coursing dogs fit in the off-season. It has grown into the largest lure-coursing association in the world. Dogs must be of an accepted sighthound breed in order to be eligible for participation. Each dog must pass a certification run in which he shows that he can run with another dog without interfering. The course is laid out using pulleys and a motor to drive the string around the pulleys. Normally white plastic bags are used as lures, although real fur strips may also be attached. Dogs run in trios, each dog handled by his own slipper. The dogs are scored on their endurance, follow, speed, agility and enthusiasm. Dogs earn their Field Champion titles by earning

Scottish Deerhound owners can take advantage of the breed's awesome speed and running power by entering their dog(s) in racing and coursing events.

two first places, or one first- and two second-place finishes, as well as accumulating 100 points. They can then go on to earn the LCM title, Lure Courser of Merit, by winning four first places and accumulating 300 additional points.

Coursing is an all-day event, held in all weather conditions. It is great fun for the whole family, but on a rainy, cold day, it's best to leave the kids at home!

## RACING

The Large Gazehound Racing Association (LGRA) and the National Oval Track Racing Association (NOTRA) are organizations that sponsor and regulate dog races. Races are usually either 200-yard sprints (LGRA) or semi- or complete ovals (NOTRA). Both of these organizations allow most sighthound breeds except Whippets to participate. (Whippets have their own racing organizations exclusively for the breed.) In both LGRA and NOTRA races, the dogs generally run out of starting boxes, meaning that racing dogs must be trained to the box. Local racing clubs offer training programs that can assist novice owners and dogs.

Dogs compete in a draw of four each and are ranked according to their previous racing record. The lure in LGRA events consists of both real fur and a predator call. In NOTRA events, the lure is white plastic and often a fur strip. There are three programs, and the dogs are rotated through the draw according to their finish in each preceding program. Dogs earn the Gazehound Racing Champion (GRC) or the Oval Racing Champion (ORC) title when they accumulate 15 race points. Dogs can go on to earn the Superior titles by accumulating 30 additional points.

Both LGRA and NOTRA races are owner-participation sports in which each owner plays some role: catcher, walker, line judge or foul judge. If you plan to race your dog, plan to work all day during a race day! There is little time for anything else, but the reward of seeing four dogs pour over the finish line shoulder to shoulder is more than enough.

And they're off! Four Deerhounds just out of the box in a racing event.

You chose your dog because something clicked the minute you set eyes on him. Or perhaps it seemed that the dog selected you and that's what clinched the deal. Either way, you are now investing time and money in this dog, a true pal and an outstanding member of the family. Everything about him is perfect—well, almost perfect. Remember, he is a dog! For that matter, how does he think *you're* doing?

**UNDERSTANDING THE CANINE MINDSET**
For starters, you and your dog are on different wavelengths. Your dog is similar to a toddler in that both live in the present tense only. A dog's view of life is based primarily on cause and effect. For example, if your dog stumbles down a flight of three steps, the next time he will likely either walk more carefully or avoid the steps altogether.

Your dog makes connections based on the fact that he lives in the present, so when he is doing something and you interrupt to dispense praise or a correction, a connection, positive or negative, is made. To the dog, that's like one plus one equals two! In the same sense, it's also easy to see that when your timing is off, you will cause an incorrect connection. The one-plus-one way of thinking is why you must never scold a dog for behavior that took place an hour, 15 minutes or even 5 seconds ago. But it is also why, when your timing is perfect, you can teach him to do all kinds of wonderful things—as soon as he has made that essential connection. What helps the process is his desire to please you and to have your approval.

There are behaviors we admire in dogs, such as friendliness and obedience, as well as those behaviors that cause problems to a varying degree. The dog owner who encounters minor behavioral problems is wise to solve them promptly or get professional help. Bad behaviors are not corrected by repeatedly shouting "No" or getting angry with the dog. Only the giving of praise and approval for good behavior lets your dog understand right from wrong. The longer a bad behavior is allowed to continue, the harder it is to overcome. A responsible breeder is often able to help. Each dog is unique, so try not to compare your dog's behavior with your neighbor's dog or the one you had as a child.

Have your veterinarian check the dog to see whether a behavior problem could have a physical cause. An earache or toothache, for example, could be the reason for a dog to snap at you if you were to touch his head when putting on his leash. A sharp correction from you would only increase the behavior. When a physical basis is eliminated, and if the problem is not something you understand or can cope with, ask for the name of a behavioral specialist, preferably one who is familiar with the Scottish Deerhound. Be sure to keep the breeder informed of your progress.

Many things, such as environment and inherited traits, form the basic behavior of a dog, just as in humans. You also must factor into his temperament the purpose for which your dog was originally bred. The major obstacle lies in the dog's inability to explain his behavior to us in a way that we understand. The one thing you should not do is to give up and abandon your dog. Somewhere a misunderstanding has occurred but, with help and patient understanding on your part, you should be able to work out the majority of bothersome behaviors.

## SEPARATION ANXIETY

Any behaviorist will tell you that separation anxiety is the most common problem about which pet owners complain. It is also one of the easiest to prevent. Unfortunately, a behaviorist usually is not consulted until the dog is a stressed-out, neurotic mess. At that stage, it is indeed a problem that requires the help of a professional.

Training the puppy to the fact that people in the house come and go is essential in order to avoid this anxiety. Leaving the puppy in his crate or a confined area while family members go in and out, and stay out for longer and longer periods of time, is the basic way to desensitize the pup to the family's frequent departures. If you are at home most of every day, make it a point to go out for at least an hour or two whenever possible.

### PROFESSIONAL HELP

Every trainer and behaviorist asks, "Why didn't you come to me sooner?" Pet owners often don't want to admit that anything is wrong with their dogs. A dog's problem often is due to the dog and his owner mixing their messages, which will only get worse. Don't put it off; consult a professional to find out whether or not the problem is serious enough to require intervention.

How you leave is vital to the dog's reaction. Your dog is no fool. He knows the difference between sweats and business suits, jeans and dresses. He sees you pat your pocket to check for your wallet, open your briefcase, check that you have your cell phone or pick up the car keys. He knows from the hurry of the kids in the morning that they're off to school until afternoon. Lipstick? Aftershave lotion? Lunch boxes? Every move you make registers in his sensory perception and memory. Your puppy knows more about your departures than you do. You can't get away with a thing!

Before you got dressed, you checked the dog's water bowl and his supply of sturdy long-lasting toys, and you turned the radio on low. You will leave him in what he considers his "safe" area, not with total freedom of the house. If you've invested in child safety gates, you can be reasonably sure that he'll remain in the designated area. Don't give him access to a window where he can watch you leave the house. If you're leaving for an hour or two, just put him into his crate with a safe toy.

Now comes the test! You are ready to walk out the door. Do not give your Scottish Deerhound a big hug and a fond farewell. Do not drag out a long goodbye. Those are the very things that jump-start separation anxiety.

Toss a biscuit into the dog's area, call out "So long, pooch" and close the door. You're gone. The chances are that the dog may bark a couple of times, or maybe whine once or twice, and then settle down to enjoy his biscuit and take a lovely nap, especially if you took him for a nice long walk before you left. As he grows up,

## I CAN'T SMILE WITHOUT YOU

How can you tell whether your dog is suffering from separation anxiety? Not every dog who enjoys a close bond with his owner will suffer from separation anxiety. In actuality, only a small percentage of dogs are affected. Separation anxiety manifests itself in dogs older than one year of age and may not occur until the dog is a senior. A number of destructive behaviors are associated with the problem, including scratch marks in front of doorways, bite marks on furniture, drool stains on furniture and flooring and tattered draperies, carpets or cushions. The most reliable sign of separation anxiety is howling and crying when the owner leaves and then barking like mad for extended periods. Affected dogs may also defecate or urinate throughout the home, attempt to escape when the door opens, vocalize excessively and show signs of depression (including loss of appetite, listlessness and lack of activity).

the barks and whines will stop because it's an old routine, so why should he make the effort?

When you first brought home the puppy, the come-and-go routine was intermittent and constant. He was put into his crate with a tiny treat. You left (silently) and returned in 3 minutes, then 5, then 10, then 15, then half an hour, until finally you could leave without a prob-lem and be gone for 2 or 3 hours. If, at any time in the future, there's a "separation" problem, refresh his memory by going back to that basic training.

Now comes the next most important part—your return. Do not make a big production of coming home. "Hi, poochie" is as grand a greeting as he needs. When you've taken off your hat and coat, tossed your briefcase on the hall table and glanced at the mail, and the dog has settled down from the excitement of seeing you "in person" from his confined area, then go and give him a warm, friendly greeting. A potty trip is needed and a walk would be appreciated, since he's been such a good dog.

## AGGRESSION
This is a problem that concerns all responsible dog owners. Aggression can be a very big prob-lem in dogs, and, when not controlled, always becomes dangerous. An aggressive dog, no

matter the size, may lunge at, bite or even attack a person or another dog. Generally, Scottish Deerhounds are not aggressive, but some males can become bitch-orientated at about two years of age. Any sign of a male's showing aggression toward other male dogs must be stopped absolutely imme-diately and firmly. The dog must be taught a lesson before bad habits form and must respect the authority of his owner.

"Aggression" is a word that is often misunderstood and is sometimes even used to describe what is actually normal canine behavior. For example, it's normal for puppies to growl when playing tug-of-war. It's puppy talk. There are different forms of dog aggression, but all are degrees of dominance, indicating that the dog, not his master, is (or thinks he is) in control. When the dog feels that he (or his control of the

Separation anxiety can cause a dog to behave as if he's suffering from a broken heart.

situation) is threatened, he will respond. The extent of the aggressive behavior varies with individual dogs. It is not at all pleasant to see bared teeth or to hear your dog growl or snarl, but these are signs of behavior that, if left uncorrected, can become extremely dangerous. A word of warning here: never challenge an aggressive dog. He is unpredictable and therefore unreliable to approach.

Nothing gets a "hello" from strangers on the street quicker than walking a puppy, but people should ask permission before petting your dog so you can tell him to sit in order to receive the admiring pats. If a hand comes down over the dog's head and he shrinks back, ask the person to bring his hand up, underneath the

**GET A WHIFF OF HIM!**
Dogs sniff each others' rears as their way of saying "hi" as well as to find out who the other dog is and how he's doing. That's normal behavior between canines, but it can, annoyingly, extend to people. The command for all unwanted sniffing is "Leave it!" Give the command in a no-nonsense voice and move on.

pup's chin. Now you're correcting strangers, too! But if you don't, it could make your dog afraid of strangers, which in turn can lead to fear-biting. Socialization prevents much aggression before it rears its ugly head.

The body language of an aggressive dog about to attack is clear. The dog will have a hard,

Aggression can stem from a dog's trying to be the dominant one in your family pack. Dogs learn pack order and etiquette at an early age through play with their littermates.

steady stare. He will try to look as big as possible by standing stiff-legged, pushing out his chest, keeping his ears up and holding his tail up and steady. The hackles on his back will rise so that a ridge of hairs stands up. This posture may include the curled lip, snarl and/or growl, or he may be silent. He looks, and definitely is, very dangerous.

This dominant posture is seen in dogs that are territorially aggressive. Deliverymen are constant victims of serious bites from such dogs. Territorial aggression is the reason you should never, ever try to train a puppy to be a watchdog. It can escalate into this type of behavior over which you will have no control. All forms of aggression must be taken seriously and dealt with immediately. If signs of aggressive behavior continue, or grow worse, or if

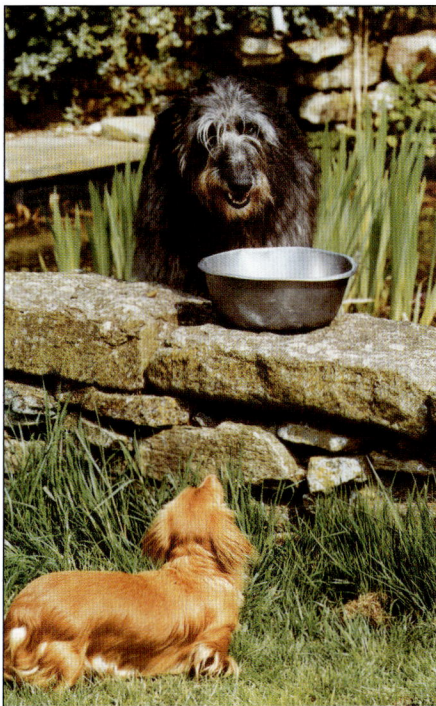

Dogs should always be introduced under supervision and given some time to get acquainted. This Scottish Deerhound and Dachshund seem like old friends, chatting around the water bowl.

you are at all unsure about how to deal with your dog's behavior, get the help of a professional.

Uncontrolled aggression, sometimes called "irritable aggression," is not something for the pet owner to try to solve. If you cannot solve your dog's dangerous behavior with professional help, and you (quite rightly) do not wish to keep a canine time-bomb in your home, you will have some important decisions to make. Aggressive dogs often cannot be rehomed successfully, as they are dangerous and unreliable in their behavior. An aggressive dog should be dealt with only by

## DOMINANCE

Dogs are born with dominance skills, meaning that they can be quite clever in trying to get their way. The "follow-me" trot to the cookie jar is an example. The toy dropped in your lap says "Play with me." The leash delivered to you along with an excited look means "Take me for a walk." These are all good-natured dominant behaviors. Ask your dog to sit before agreeing to his request and you'll remain "top dog."

## ONE BITE TOO MANY

It's natural for puppies to bite in play, but you must teach your puppy that this is unacceptable in human circles. Relax your hand, say "No bite" and offer him a toy. An adolescent dog is testing his dominance and will bite as a way of disobeying you. If not stopped in puppyhood, you will end up with an adult dog that will bite aggressively. All adult biting should be considered serious and dealt with by a professional.

someone who knows exactly the situation that he is getting into and has the experience with the breed, dedication and ideal living environment to attempt rehabilitating the dog, which may not even be possible. In these cases, the dog ends up having to be humanely put down. Making a decision about euthanasia is not an easy undertaking for anyone, for any reason, but you cannot pass on to another home a dog that you know could cause harm.

A milder form of aggression is the dog's guarding anything that he perceives to be his—his food dish, his toys, his bed and/or his crate. This can be prevented if you take firm control from the start. The young puppy can and should be taught that his leader will share, but that certain rules apply. Guarding is mild aggression only in the beginning stages,

and it will worsen and become dangerous if you let it.

Don't try to snatch anything away from your puppy. Bargain for the item in question so that you can positively reinforce him when he gives it up. Punishment only results in worsening any aggressive behavior.

Many dogs extend their guarding impulse toward items they've stolen. The dog figures, "If I have it, it's mine!" (Some ill-behaved kids have similar tendencies.) An angry confrontation will only increase the dog's aggression. (Have you ever watched a child have a tantrum?) Try a simple distraction first, such as tossing a toy or picking up his leash for a walk. If that doesn't work, the best way to handle the situation is with basic obedience. Show the dog a treat, followed by calm, almost slow-motion commands: "Come. Sit. Drop it. Good dog," and then hand over the cheese! That's one example of positive-reinforcement training.

Children can be bitten when they try to retrieve a stolen shoe or toy, so they need to know how to handle the dog or to let an adult do it. They may also be bitten as they run away from a dog, in either fear or play. The dog sees the child's running as reason for pursuit, and even a friendly young puppy will nip at the heels of a runaway. Teach the kids not to run away from a strange dog and when to stop overly exciting play with their own puppy.

Fear biting is yet another aggressive behavior. A fear biter gives many warning signals. The dog leans away from the approaching person (sometimes hiding behind his owner) with his ears and tail down, but not in submission. He may even shiver. His hackles are raised, his lips curled. When the person steps into the dog's "flight zone" (a circle of 1 to 3 feet surrounding the dog), he attacks. Because of the fear factor, he performs a rapid attack-and-retreat. Because it is directed at a person, vets are often the victims of this form of aggression. It is frightening, but discovering and eliminating the cause of the fright will help overcome the dog's need to bite. Early socialization again plays a strong role in

What a big toy...and all for me! You'd be surprised at what your pup finds chewable, especially if bored or not given enough activity.

the prevention of this behavior. Again, if you can't cope with it, get the help of an expert.

## CHEWING

All puppies chew. All dogs chew. This is a fact of life for canines, and sometimes you may think it's what your dog does best! A pup starts chewing when his first set of teeth erupts and continues throughout the teething period. Chewing gives the pup relief from itchy gums and incoming teeth and, from that time on, he gets great satisfaction out of this normal, somewhat idle, canine activity. Providing safe chew toys is the best way to direct this behavior in an appropriate manner. Chew toys are available

### DOGS OF PREY

Chasing small animals is in the blood of many dogs, perhaps most; they think that this is a fun recreational activity (although some are more likely to bring you an undesirable "gift" as a result of the hunt). The good old "Leave it" command works to deter your dog from taking off in pursuit of "prey," but only if taught with the dog on leash for control. The same goes for chasing cars and bicycles.

in all sizes, textures and flavors, but you must monitor the wear-and-tear inflicted on your pup's toys to be sure that the ones you've chosen are safe and remain in good condition.

Puppies cannot distinguish between a rawhide toy and a nice leather shoe or wallet. It's up to you to keep your possessions

## THE MACHO DOG

The Venus/Mars differences are found in dogs, too. Males have distinct behaviors that, while seemingly sex-related, are more closely connected to the role of the male as leader. Marking territory by urinating on it is one means that male dogs use to establish their presence. Doing so merely says, "I've been here." Small dogs often attempt to lift their legs higher on the tree than the previous male. While this is natural behavior outdoors on items like telephone poles, fence posts, fire hydrants and most other upright objects, marking indoors is totally unacceptable. Treat it as you would a house-training accident and clean thoroughly to eradicate the scent.

Another behavior often seen in the macho male, mounting is a dominance display. Neutering the dog before six months of age helps to deter this behavior. You can discourage him from mounting by catching the dog as he's about to mount you, stepping quickly aside and saying "Off!"

away from the dog and to keep your eye on the dog. There's a form of destruction caused by chewing that is not the dog's fault. Let's say you allow him on the sofa. One day he takes a rawhide bone up on the sofa and, in the course of chewing on the bone, takes up a bit of fabric. He continues to chew. Disaster! Now you've learned the lesson: dogs with chew toys have to be either kept off furniture and carpets, carefully supervised or put into their confined areas for chew time.

The wooden legs of furniture are favorite objects for chewing. The first time, tell the dog "Leave it!" (or "No!") and offer him a chew toy as a substitute. But your clever dog may be hiding under the chair and doing some silent destruction, which you may not notice until it's too late. In this case, it's time to try one of the foul-tasting products, made specifically to prevent destructive chewing, that is sprayed on the objects of your dog's chewing attention. These products also work to keep the dog away from plants, trash, etc. It's even a good way to stop the dog from "mouthing" or chewing on your hands or the leg of your pants. (Be sure to wash your hands after the mouthing lesson!) A little spray goes a long way.

## JUMPING UP
Jumping up is a device of enthusiastic, attention-seeking puppies,

but adult dogs often like to jump up as well, usually as a form of canine greeting. This is a controversial issue. Some owners wouldn't have it any other way! They encourage their dogs, and the owners and dogs alike enjoy the friendly physical contact. Some owners think that it's cute when it comes from a puppy, but not from an adult.

Conversely, there are those who consider jumping up to be one of the worst kinds of bad manners to be found in a dog, and others who are intimidated by such a large dog's jumping up. There are two situations in which your dog should be restrained from any and all jumping up. One is around children, especially young children and those who are not at ease with dogs. The other is when you are entertaining guests. No one who comes dressed up for a party wants to be groped by your dog, no matter how friendly his intentions or how clean his paws.

The answer to this one is relatively simple. If the dog has already started to jump up, the first command is "Off," followed immediately by "Sit." The dog must sit every time you are about to meet a friend on the street or when someone enters your home, be it child or adult. You may have to ask people to ignore the dog for a few minutes in order to let his urge for an enthusiastic greeting

subside. If your dog is too exuberant and won't sit still, you'll have to work harder by first telling him "Off" and then issuing the down/stay command. This requires more work on your part because the down is a submissive position, and your dog is only trying to be super-friendly. A small treat is expected when training for this particular down.

If you have a real pet peeve about a dog's jumping up, then disallow it from the day your puppy comes home. Jumping up is a subliminally taught human-to-dog greeting. Dogs don't greet each other in this way. It begins because your puppy is close to the ground, and he's easier to pet and cuddle if he reaches up and you

**DIGGING OUT**
Some dogs love to dig. Others wouldn't think of it. Digging is considered "self-rewarding behavior" because it's fun! Of all the digging solutions offered by the experts, most are only marginally successful and none are guaranteed to work. The best cure is prevention, which means removing the dog from the offending site when he digs as well as distracting him when you catch him digging so that he turns his attentions elsewhere. That means that you have to supervise your dog's yard time. An unsupervised digger can create havoc with your landscaping or, worse, run away!

bend over to meet him halfway. If you won't like it later, don't start it when he is young, but do give lots of praise and affection for a good sit.

## BARKING

Scottish Deerhounds can be vocal as puppies. As adults, however, they do not bark in the way that the scenthound breeds do, and they are certainly not guard dogs. However, Scottish Deerhounds do howl, although rarely for long. Times at which they howl particularly are when a bitch is in season, when they are waiting for a walk or when there is a full moon.

If you have a rare Scottish Deerhound who has too much to say about everything he sees, hears, smells and thinks he sees, hears and smells, then this habitual barker must be taught to quiet down. Such excessive barking is a problem that should be corrected early on, as soon as it surfaces in the puppy. As your Scottish Deerhound grows up, you will be able to tell when his barking is purposeful and when it is for no reason. You will become able to distinguish between your dog's different barks and their meanings. For example, the bark when someone comes to the door will be different from the bark when he is excited to see you. It is similar to a person's tone of voice, except that the dog has to rely totally on tone of voice because he does not have the benefit of using words. An incessant barker will be evident at an early age.

There are some things that encourage a dog to bark. For example, if your dog barks nonstop for a few minutes and you give him a treat to quiet him, he believes that you are rewarding him for barking. He will associate barking with getting a treat and will keep doing it until he is rewarded. On the other hand, if you give him a command such as "Quiet" and praise him after he has stopped barking for a few seconds, he will get the idea that being "quiet" is what you want him to do.

If someone coming up your driveway or to your door provokes a barking frenzy, use the saturation method to stop it. Have several friends come and go every

### PANHANDLING POOCHES

If there's one thing at which dogs excel, it is begging. If there's one thing that owners lack, it's the willpower to resist giving in to their canine beggars! If you don't give in to your adorable puppy, he won't grow into an adult dog that's a nuisance. However, give in just once and the dog will forever figure, "maybe this time." Treats are rewards for correct performance, a category into which begging definitely does not fall.

three or four minutes over as long a period of time as they can spare (it could take a couple of hours). Attach about a foot of rope to the dog's collar and have very small treats handy. Each time a car pulls up or a person approaches, let the dog bark once (grab the rope if you need to physically restrain him), say "Okay, good dog," give him a treat and make him sit. "Okay" is the release command. It lets the dog know that he has alerted you and tells him that you are now in charge. That person leaves and the next arrives, and so on and so on until everyone—especially the dog—is bored and the barking has stopped. Don't forget to thank your friends. Your neighbors, by the way, may be more than willing to assist you in this parlor game if it means a quiet dog on the block.

There is one more kind of vocalizing, which is called "idiot barking" (from *idiopathic*, meaning of unknown cause). It is usually rhythmic or a timed series of barks. Put a stop to it immediately by calling the dog to come. This form of barking can drive neighbors crazy and commonly occurs when a dog is left outside for long periods of time. He is completely and thoroughly bored! A change of scenery may help, such as relocating him to a room indoors when he is used to being outside. A few new toys or different dog biscuits might be the solu-

tion. If he is left alone while you are at work and no one can get home during the day, a noontime walk with a local dog-sitter would be the perfect solution.

Although not known as incessant barkers, Scottish Deerhounds do sometimes howl, and some have more to say than others.

## STOP, THIEF!

The easiest way to prevent a dog from stealing food is to stop this behavior before it starts by never leaving food out where he can reach it. However, if it is too late and your dog has already made a steal, you must stop your furry felon from becoming a repeat offender. Once Sneaky Pete has successfully stolen food, place a bit of food where he can reach it. Place an empty soda can with some pebbles in it on top of the food. Leave the room and watch what happens. As the dog grabs the tasty morsel, the can comes with it. The noise of the tumbling pebble-filled can makes its own correction, and you don't have to say a word.

# INDEX

Page numbers in **boldface** indicate illustrations.

# My Scottish Deerhound

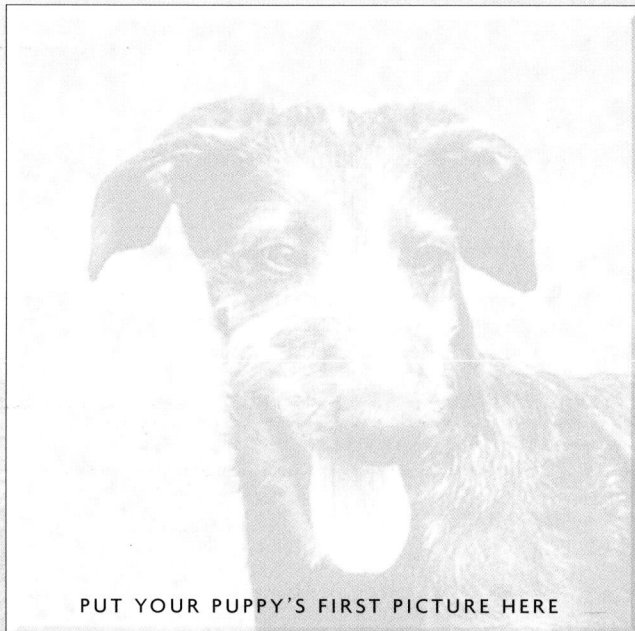

PUT YOUR PUPPY'S FIRST PICTURE HERE

Dog's Name _____

Date _____ Photographer _____